FROM FIELDS
TO COURTS

JUDGE JAMES V. PIERCE

To order additional copies of this book, contact:
Xlibris
1-888-795-4274
www.Xlibris.com
Orders@Xlibris.com
759584

Foreword

My story started on a Sunday morning in Dunedin, Florida with birds chirping and sounds of the waterfall flowing. Almost two days after being re-elected as a Pinellas County Judge for a third term, I am inspired to share my life's journey and some of the valuable lessons I learned from the many people, places, things and situations I experienced along the way. I found that the secret of being happy is doing things for other people. A life is not important except for the impact it has on the lives of others. Whatever success you achieve, pour it out to others and you will find happiness.

On May 4, 2014, I started thinking about a speech I had agreed to give at the 100 Black Men of Valdosta Black Tie Gala. While speaking engagements are common for many judges, this one was especially significant for me. It would be the first time that I had ever been a keynote speaker in my home town, Valdosta, Georgia, affectionately referred to by several names including: the Azalea City/ Winnersville, or Title Town, USA.

I thought of my life experiences, how I entered the world, and arrived at my status in life today. There are many stories to tell. This is my story of how a poor country boy from Valdosta went from the fields of South Georgia to become a judge for the courts of the 6th Judicial Circuit in Pinellas County Florida. It is my hope that the readers may gain some valuable insight about important lessons for life which I learned on my life's journey from the field to the court.

Contents

Chapter One

RESPECT

Every day I go to work with a smile and pray for wisdom to make prudent decisions, and respect everyone. As I demonstrate respect and civility toward all persons coming before me, I require similar conduct from others. After serving 4 years in the County Court Criminal Division of the 6th Judicial Circuit, the following proceedings took place during a court hearing.

THE COURT: Next up is Paul Smith; State your name.

THE DEFENDANT: Paul Smith

THE COURT: Mr. Smith, you have a charge of violation of pretrial release. You have no bond set in your case. Are you still living at 1015 River Road South, Clearwater, Florida?

THE DEFENDANT: Yes, sir but I would like to – I would like to move today. I would like – I'm going to move to St. Petersburg. Can we have this dismissed so I can get my stuff and move? The complainant made a written request for the charges to be dropped.

THE COURT: No. Are you going to hire an attorney?

THE DEFENDANT: No, sir.

THE COURT: Okay. I'll appoint the PD [Public Defender] to represent you.

What says the State regarding his bond?

ASSISTANT STATE ATTORNEY: Your Honor, I did not speak with the victim in this case. I'm not aware of anything that the defendant just said. Unfortunately, I had a wrong number.

The date of offense for the domestic battery that he's violating his pretrial release was May 4, in which he was ordered to have no contact. Additionally, he has a 2004 aggravated assault that was a No Information, (Prosecution decided to not file a criminal charge) a 2004 grand theft in which he served jail time, a '98 trespass. Most importantly, he had a '98 aggravated assault, aggravated stalking, carrying a concealed firearm, which he was sentenced to six years and four months {Department of Corrections} DOC. I think he ended up serving five years DOC.

I'd ask for at least a $7,500 bond.

THE COURT: All right. I'm going to set your bond at $10,000.

THE DEFENDANT: Hey, Your Honor, the State had Karen's written statement today. I'm being prosecuted, when all I did was try to stop her from hitting me in the face.

THE COURT: All right. Well, talk to your lawyer about it.

ASSISTANT STATE ATTORNEY: And Your Honor, the new charge – the domestic battery, if we could revoke that bond and set a new bond.

THE DEFENDANT: Yeah, she's got so many – she's got so many facts wrong. It wasn't five years in prison; it was 6.4 years. I mean, it's just ridiculous. Why am I being prosecuted when you have written proof that these charges should be dismissed?

ASSISTANT PUBLIC DEFENDER: Mr. Smith – Mr. Smith--

THE DEFENDANT: And I should have a reasonable bail. I'm constitutionally entitled to one.

THE COURT: What's the bond on – okay, what was the bond on the battery?

ASSISTANT STATE ATTORNEY: Thirty-five hundred, Your Honor.

THE COURT: Okay. Revoke that $3,500 bond and set that at $10,000.

THE CLERK: What's the case number?

THE COURT: You got a case number, State?

ASSISTANT STATE ATTORNEY: Yes, your honor. It's CTC ---

THE DEFENDANT: (Profanity directed toward the court)

THE COURT: All right sir. I'm going to hold you in direct contempt of Court.

THE DEFENDANT: (profanity directed to the court)

THE COURT: All right.

UNIDENTIFIED SPEAKER: Why you doing that, man?

THE DEFENDANT: (More profanity directed to the court)

UNIDENTIFIED SPEAKER: You're making him mad. You're messing everybody else up, man.

THE BAILIFF: All right, stop talking.

THE BAILIFF: Go on, please, your honor.

THE COURT: Let me see that affidavit {sworn statement} again.

THE DEFENDANT: (More profanity directed to court)

THE COURT: Hold on. Don't take him out yet. Bring him back, Deputy.

THE BAILIFF: Yes, sir.

THE COURT: Bring him back.

THE DEFENDANT: (more profanity) Prosecuting me when you know you shouldn't be. You scumbag!

THE COURT: All right, Mr. Smith.

THE DEFENDANT: What? (more profanity directed to the court.)

THE COURT: At this point I'm going to appoint the Public Defender's Office to represent you for contempt of court.

THE DEFENDANT: Good. Good. (More profanity directed to court.)

THE COURT: All right. So at this point I'll hold you in contempt of court.

THE DEFENDANT: (More profanity directed to the court.) I don't care what you do.

THE COURT: Okay.

THE DEFENDANT: Okay.

THE COURT: You done?

THE DEFENDANT: Yeah, I'm done, (profanity). I don't even want to talk to you. (more profanity directed to the court)

ASSISTANT STATE ATTORNEY: Judge –

THE DEFENDANT: Okay. It should be dismissed. (More profanity directed to the court.)

THE COURT: Is there anything else you want to say at this time?

THE BAILIFF: Stop talking.

THE COURT: Anything else you want to say?

THE DEFENDANT: No, I'm done. I got it out of me. Thanks. Have a nice day.

THE COURT: Okay. Now, it's my time to talk.

THE DEFENDANT: Okay.

THE COURT: Now, is there any reason why I should not hold you in contempt of court for insulting the Court in open court and making those other comments that you just made?

THE DEFENDANT: Yes, sir.

THE COURT: And what are those?

THE DEFENDANT: Because you're prosecuting me when I should not be prosecuted.

THE COURT: Okay. Anything else you want to say?

THE DEFENDANT: Yes. The charges should have been dismissed and I should have been released today. And you know that full well.

THE COURT: Anything else?

THE DEFENDANT: No, sir.

THE COURT: All right. I'm going to hold you in contempt of the Court and sentence you to five months and 29 days in the Pinellas County Jail. Have a good day, sir.

THE DEFENDANT: Thank you, sir.

While not every day on the bench is like the incident above, there are certain defining moments which remain memorable. Needless to say, this was one of them. Former 6th Judicial Circuit chief Judge Susan Schaffer advised judges to be careful about holding lawyers in contempt of court, but she had no reservations about holding a defendant in contempt of court. Contempt of court, often referred to simply as "contempt," is the offense of being disobedient to or disrespectful towards a court of law and its officers in the form of behavior that opposes or defies authority, justice, and dignity of the court. Contempt of court is the judge's strongest power to impose sanctions for acts that disrupt the court's normal process. The Principles of Professionalism for Florida Judges state that a judge should maintain control of the proceedings, recognizing that judges have both the obligation and authority to insure that all proceedings are conducted in a civil and respectful manner.

The defendant's lack of respect for the court resulted in him being held in contempt of court. Despite the defendant's rudeness and disrespect, I maintained my composure and conducted his hearing in a civil and respectful manner. Respect for authority is one of the most important values to teach a child. A child's parent is the first teacher of love, obedience, and respect. If children disrespect their parents, they will have no respect for themselves or anyone else.

Respect for others results in good manners and self-respect produces discipline and self–control. While it is important to receive respect, it is equally important to give respect. If you treat others the way you want to be treated, you will be successful in both your personal and professional relationships. It is impossible to love another person without respect. Respect is one of the greatest expressions of love in humanity.

Chapter Two

Roots

My maternal great- great- great - grandmother was an American Indian probably from the Cherokee Tribe which inhabited Watauga County, North Carolina. Her name is unknown but she was a mistress to a white plantation owner. My maternal great -great- grandparents were David and Mary Morse. My grandmother would often talk about her heritage. Her yellow skin and high cheek bone structure represented her American Indian heritage. That same cheek bone structure would play a part in receiving my college marching band freshman nickname, "Apache."

My Maternal great - grandfather, Simon Johnson, was listed in the U.S. Census of 1890 as a wagon driver and married Alice Morse, my maternal great grandmother, on April 23, 1872 in Lowndes County, Georgia. My maternal grandmother, (Fannie Bell) born October 23, 1898, was the youngest of 14 siblings.

One of the most important ways to live a happy life is developing and nourishing meaningful relationships. Relationships are the building blocks of a meaningful life. Love is the concrete that holds those relationships together. Charity begins at home with family and I was blessed to have a wonderful, kind and gentle mother along with four maternal siblings who experienced the same nurturing and loving care.

My mother, Leola Padilla, was a God fearing woman and the daughter of Mr. and Mrs. Sherman Morrell Sr. and they loved the Lord.

My mother and grandparents did not consume alcoholic beverages and their integrity and character transcended their poverty.

I was fortunate to grow up in my grandparents' home. Every grandchild and great grandchild called my grandparents "Momma and Daddy." My maternal grandmother and grandfather were married in 1910 and were together for 62 years until he died in 1972. Their love for each other resulted in ten offspring. Grandmother loved the ground that Grandfather walked on and attended to all his needs in sickness and health. Breakfast, lunch and dinner was a daily routine with her other housekeeping and domestic tasks. Sherman's dinner would always be ready for him when he returned from a day of plowing fields with his mule and wagon.

My grandparents were two very extraordinary people who lived typical ordinary lives in Lowndes County, Georgia. My grandfather, born in 1892, had no formal education, but was able to write his name. He was a farmer and well respected for his agricultural skills.

On more than one occasion, I remember entering my grandfather's sugar cane in the Lowndes County Fair 4-H {head, heart, hands, health} exhibits through my school, Wetherington – Robinson. I always received blue ribbon awards for my entries. The stout stalks of both red and green juicy sugar cane ranged from six to 12 feet tall. My grandfather knew exactly how to space the plants for optimal growth and when to harvest them to avoid frost damage from severe cold weather. My favorite time of the year was when the cane was harvested and driven on my grandfather's mule and wagon to our neighbor, Mrs. McDougal, for grinding.

The cane would then be fed through a grinder which was powered by the mule continuously pulling a lever around a circle that was connected to a grinder. The stalks of sugar cane would be inserted into the cane grinder which squeezed the juice from the stalk. The cane juice was cooked in a large basin under a furnace until it became syrup. Cane grinding requires expertise, hard work and long hours for a small payoff. A 10th of an acre of cane produces about 60 gallons of juice. Sixty gallons of juice might boil down to six gallons of thick amber syrup. The sweet aroma of syrup cooking in a large basin furnace remains indelibly impressed in my fondest childhood memories. The cane grinding and cooking was a social event where neighbors would gather, share stories and jokes well into the night.

Although money was scarce, our family never went hungry. My grandfather always had a garden filled with all the traditional staples including corn, okra, tomatoes, cabbage, collard greens, turnip greens, cucumbers, squash, butter beans, peas and the sweetest watermelons and cantaloupes you could imagine. Pink and red watermelons and red and green cane were his signature crops. Looking back, it was amazing that my grandfather grew all these things without a tractor but with a mule, plow, and horse manure for fertilizer.

Sherman Morrell was not only a great farmer but he loved hunting and trapping. He would set steel traps for foxes and sell the hides. Often he would bring home wild game including quails, raccoons, possum, rabbits and squirrels which he had trapped or killed with his 12 gauge shot gun. He would also raise hogs and chickens which provided our daily staple of meat for breakfast and dinner.

My grandmother was a resilient Christian whom lived her faith through her words and good deeds. She joined Irvin Hill Baptist Church at an early age and faithfully served until her health failed. The scripture tells us to "honor your mother and father so things will go well with you and your days will be long upon the earth." This is one of the most important life lessons to know and one which was often emphasized by my grandmother. She would often say, "Nothing good will become of a disobedient child." She had great respect for her mother and father. Perhaps this explains her longevity of 97 years of life. She survived double leg amputations but succumbed to kidney failure on her way to glory on April 19, 1996. Fannie Bell Morrell was not only our family's matriarch, but she was a mother to every boy, girl, woman or man that found themselves in her presence.

Despite only having a second grade education, she was well informed about politics and other current issues. Most importantly, Grandmother emphasized to me and many others, the value of an education. She would often say, "Boy get your education because it's something that no one can take away from you." I have repeated her sage remark to many young people and it remains one of the most inspiring ideas Grandmother gave to me.

She would never let a grandchild or any child leave her home without giving them something before they left. It might be an apple or orange or a nickel or dime but you were guaranteed to leave her with more than you had on arrival. As a child growing up, if I needed money for anything, I could go to her and be assured that if Grandmother had it she would give it to me. Another important lesson for life that I learned from my grandmother: "It is always better to give than to receive."

One more thing about grandmother, she loved watching professional wrestling. On any given Saturday afternoon, you could hear her yelling and shouting for her favorite wrestler, "Beat him, hit him, I hope you beat the mess out of that ole nasty rascal." Grandmother was a true fan of wrestling and she wanted the good guys to win.

We did not have an automobile; although I learned at some point in my grandfather's life, he did buy a truck which was driven by his son, my Uncle David. On more than one occasion, my grandfather would take me to the fields with him where he picked corn and cucumbers. My job was to drive the mule and wagon as he loaded the corn unto the wagon.

As a small boy, steering a mule was an enormous feat. Grandfather would say, "Don't let the mule know you are afraid." Both the mule and I knew that there was no way I could stop her once she started moving. I told my grandfather that I couldn't stop the mule because she was much stronger than me. His response was: "There's no such word as can't." Although I did not quite understand what my grandfather meant as a child, it would later make perfectly good sense to me.

As a child, I took what he said literally but now I understand the life lesson was that whatever you can conceive, and believe, you can achieve. All things are possible, if you have faith and confidence. This lesson of trust and confidence would carry me from the fields of South Georgia to the courtrooms of Pinellas County, Florida.

My grandfather was a well -respected man in Lowndes County and a deacon at Morning Star Baptist Church. To this day, there are people who still remember Mr. Sherman Morrell. He would only ride in the front seat when he was a passenger in an automobile. I am uncertain whether his seat preference was a result of pride or self-esteem. Perhaps he just wanted to have the best view to his destination. Grandfather loved smoking his pipe, and whenever I smell pipe tobacco I think of my grandfather, Sherman Morrell.

My grandfather worked hard and provided well for our family. He raised chickens and hogs and made many jars of syrup from his sugar cane crops. Each winter he would slaughter a hog for meat. Like most our neighbors, we did not have the luxuries of central heating and running water with faucets. We had an outhouse (outdoor toilet), a manual water pump outside, and a fireplace which was the primary source of heat for the winter until our landlord installed a gas heater. Every meal was cooked on an iron stove with wood which also provided heat in the winter time.

Our home was quite small and my mother along with my younger brother and I shared a bedroom with my grandmother and grandfather until we moved our bed into the living room when the gas heater was installed. We shared my grandmother and grandfather's bedroom because the fireplace was located there and it kept us warm during the freezing South Georgia winter nights. Our home only had three rooms. The third room was where my sisters slept until they left home. They would usually warm their covers in front of the fireplace and then rush them to their beds because there was no heat in the back room. Our wooden house had a tin roof and was very cold with no insulation. The cold windy drafts permeated the cracks around the doors and walls.

My grandfather was a disciplinarian and there were many occasions when my siblings and I received a thrashing. On one occasion, I recalled taking my cousin, Amos, also my best friend growing up and pretending to hold him hostage. I have no idea what motivated me to do such a thing other than I really liked my cousin and did not want him to leave. Knowing that I was going to be punished by grandfather, I decided to stay outside until it turned dark. Then it was time to reap what I had sowed and he did not spare the rod which I really deserved. Grandfather was the type of father who only needed to look at you to stop your misbehaving.

SHERMAN MORRELL

GREAT GRANDMOTHER ALICE MORSE JOHNSON

Our lives changed when we arrived home on a cold Saturday night after going shopping in Valdosta with my sister Pearl and my brother –in-law, Shorty (William Henry Wright). We found Grandfather lying on the wood pile behind our house after suffering a debilitating stroke. The stroke ended his career as a farmer and bread winner. He lost the use of an arm and ultimately died from throat cancer in the summer of 1972. Unfortunately, I was unable to attend his funeral because of being bed ridden with the flu. His death affected me both physically and emotionally. I was now the oldest male in our home and felt I needed to do everything possible to help my mother, grandmother and younger brother.

James V. Pierce

My grandparents, Mr. & Mrs. Sherman Morrell,
my brother Joseph Padilla

Chapter Three

MADEAR

My maternal grandparents bore ten children: Eugene, Essie Mae, Lillar Mae, Sherman Jr., Leola, Robert, David and Elizabeth and two that died in infancy. Leola, whom my siblings and I called "Madear," was born January 19, 1929 during the same year and month as civil rights leader, Dr. Martin Luther King, Jr. Several months later, in March of 1929, my mentor and professor at Bethune-Cookman College, Dr. Jake Miller was born. Each of them would have a significant impact on my life.

MRS. LEOLA PADILLA

My mother, Leola Padilla, was a quiet spirit with a very kind heart. She only got angry when my younger brother and I were misbehaving and that was not often. I don't remember her ever using corporal punishment or any kind of punishment on us because of our mischief. Likewise, I cannot remember her having any physical or verbal confrontation with anyone. She was a beautiful woman both inside and out. Her 5'8" slender stature, glistening long hair and smooth pecan tan complexion would definitely attract a man's attention. My siblings and I called her "Madear."

MADEAR AND I

Leola attended Dasher High School in Lowndes County through the tenth grade and spent most, if not all of her working days doing agricultural work. She would work as a tobacco handler and picked cotton, corn and cucumbers. In the spring, she would pick peaches, and go into the woods to gather a leafy vegetation known as deer- tongue in Kroger sacks.

The leafy vegetation was blended with tobacco and can be found in marshy ground, thickets, wood margins and roadsides. I would often accompany Madear into the woods around our house to find deer- tongue growing wildly. Sometime during the week, a buyer would come through, weigh it and purchase it for about 21 cents per pound. Madear worked very hard performing various agricultural work in the blazing South Georgia sun to make ends meet as a single parent of five children. We are eternally grateful for her toil and labor of love. She made many sacrifices for her children to have the basic essentials of life.

Madear would often sit us on her lap and help us learn to read our first grade Alice & Jerry book. She would also encourage us to save some of our summer earnings by asking us, "What will we have saved when ole Jack Frost arrives?" She understood the importance of teaching us some economic sense. She gave her children all of her love and a good moral compass to be successful in life. She would take us to Sunday-School and Church and I never heard her swear or use profanity. She believed in the Lord and I am confident that she is rejoicing in heaven with the believers.

Madear married Alfred Anderson in the mid-1940s and conceived my older siblings Alfred Jr., Pearl and Helen. Unfortunately, unpleasant circumstances of alcohol abuse, infidelity and neglect resulted in Madear leaving Alfred and getting divorced. Alfred would later spend a significant portion of his life incarcerated in the Georgia State prison for committing a homicide until his release during the late seventies. The details of this incident are unclear but Madear said he stabbed a man after an argument over gambling. Madear and Alfred would reunite while I was away in college and live together until his passing.

When I was about three years old, my mother married Joseph Padilla who was Mexican and my youngest brother's father. After moving to Lansing, Michigan, we lived in the basement of my Uncle Robert and his wife's home. Joseph loved to play the accordion and was apt at repairing automobiles and appliances. Unfortunately, Joseph had an argument with a man about his tools and killed him.

My stepfather fled after the homicide and was later arrested in Toledo, Ohio. We believe he was deported to Mexico. We never saw him again and my youngest brother, Joseph, was born after my mother and I returned to Valdosta. Joseph had curly hair like his father and we loved our little brother. My sisters doted over him like they did with me and I was glad to have a little brother.

Despite the negative circumstances surrounding my older sibling's upbringing, each of them grew up to become productive citizens and the best brother and sisters imaginable. Alfred and Helen retired from the automotive industry in Lansing, Michigan as did many other family members who migrated north for employment and a better standard of living in the late 60s and early 70s. Pearl, my oldest sister, found a job as a respiratory therapist and spent more than 40 years at South Georgia Medical Center where she matriculated to a supervisor and retired.

My family, Pearl, Mother Leola, Helen, Alfred, Joe and I

Chapter Four

HOMETOWN

If you are driving north on Interstate 75, Lowndes County is the first county you enter after crossing the Florida/Georgia state line. If you take exit 16, you will end up in the heart of Valdosta which is one of the largest cities in South Georgia. The local economy received an important boost when Interstate 75 was routed and built through the area. Many vacationers on their way to Florida found Valdosta a convenient "last stop" on their way to Walt Disney World and the Orlando area, especially those coming from the north. President George W. Bush received his National Guard flight training at Valdosta's Moody Air Force Base in November 1968.

Valdosta and Lowndes County football programs are recognized throughout the state and nationally for their winning traditions. The Valdosta High Wildcats have the winningest football program in the entire country. Some of the Valdosta and Lowndes County alumni have made major impacts in college and professional football. The Florida Gator fans will always remember a quarterback from Valdosta, Georgia who played for the Georgia Bulldogs and threw the game winning 93 yard touchdown pass to receiver, Lindsey Scott, in the 1980 Florida/Georgia game.

Benjamin Franklin "Buck" Belue played American football and baseball at the University of Georgia from 1978 to 1981. He played quarterback for the Georgia Bulldogs in 1980 when the team went 12-0, and won a national championship after beating Notre Dame in the Sugar Bowl. The Valdosta High School Wildcats have one of the most successful high school football programs in the country with six national championships (1962, 1969, 1971, 1984, 1986, 1992), 24 Georgia state championships between 1940 and 2016, and 41 region titles. Most of those victories occurred under the coaching legends, Wright Bazemore and Nick Hyder.

The annual matchup between Lowndes and Valdosta High School is known as the Winnersville Classic. My alma mater, Lowndes County High School (LHS) Vikings, has also built a strong program, winning five state titles since 1980. Lowndes County High's first victory against Valdosta occurred in 1977, the year after I graduated from LHS. After experiencing nine consecutive losing seasons to Valdosta High, Lowndes County High defeated the Wildcats in a historic victory by a score of 7 to 2 under coaching legend, Joe Wilson. The Valdosta University Blazers have won a total of three Division III national titles (2004, 2007 and 2012). We are Winnersville!

Chapter Five

God's Plan -What's in a name?

My conception circumstances may raise an eye brow but shows how God's omnipotent power works to accomplish his plan:

"Before I formed thee in the belly I knew thee; and before thou cometh forth out of the womb I sanctified thee, and I ordained thee a prophet unto the nations." Jeremiah 1:4 KJV

Entering the world as a result of promiscuity may not be ideal, but giving an opportunity to enter the world and live well is a gift from God. My life experience did not begin under an optimal set of circumstances. The facts and circumstances of how my mother and Willie B. Pierce conceived me are probably too salacious to discuss and better yet just left alone. I am fortunate because God had a plan to make a poor, rural, black child born out of wedlock into a judge for the 6th Judicial Circuit of Pinellas County.

To say my father was a "rolling stone" would be an understatement. I never bonded with my father and never had any significant father/son time with him. Willie B. Pierce was married and father of four other children at the time of my birth. I was born December 16, 1958 in a tin roof house on what was once a dirt road in rural Lowndes County. My paternal half - brother, Benjamin, share the same year of birth with me and we attended the same middle and high school along with my paternal half-sister, Wendolyn. I have always gotten along well with my paternal siblings. We respect each other and have become closer over the years. Even though my mother and father were never married, I feel fortunate to have received his last name even though no birth certificate was completed at the time of my birth.

Occasionally, I would see Willie B. at the barbershop and he would give my mother money for my haircut. Other than one other visit as a child to his marital home, I had no other significant interaction with him. I cried while visiting his home. It was not because I was mistreated; it was because I missed the comfort and love of the people that I knew as my family. I never felt any hostility toward Willie B. like many other children probably experienced under similar circumstances.

I started school at Wetherington - Robinson Elementary in fall of 1963. At that time, nine years had passed since the United States Supreme Court had decided **Brown vs. the Topeka Kansas Board of Education** when it determined that separate school systems for blacks and whites were not equal. Nevertheless, our school system in Lowndes County remained segregated like most throughout the country. Our school system would remain segregated until Fall of 1969.

Ms. Ola, my first grade teacher asked me my name.

I said, "My name is J.V. Pierce."

She asked, "What does the J. and V. stand for?"

I did not know and was instructed to ask my mother what J.V. stood for. Upon inquiry with my mother, I was told that my name is J.V. Pierce and I was named after my uncle. With this information now confirmed, I boldly told Ms. Ola, "My name is J.V. Pierce. Once again Ms. Ola said, "You cannot have initials for your name!"

Unlike most other first graders, I did not have a birth certificate. My date of birth and name was recorded in our family bible. "Madear, the teacher said I couldn't have a full name with just initials." Madear told me I was named after Uncle J.V., or J.B. depending on which family member you were asking. She thought the J stood for James but was unsure what the V stood for. I was not about to face Ms. Ola without knowing my full name. I decided to take the middle name of Vincent after the renowned moderator and entertainer, Vincent Price. From that day forward I would be James Vincent Pierce.

My most vivid memory of first grade was sitting at what was called the "cow tail." The end of the table was for the slow learners and I was at the very end. It probably did not help to be only five years old when I started first grade and most of my classmates were six or turning six after school started. One thing I knew for sure, I did not like school and being the "cow tail."

Some days I would pretend to have misplaced my shoes, so I would miss the bus and not have to attend school. I was fortunate to have my older brother, Alfred Jr., who taught me my ABCs and help me to make it out of first grade. The same big brother who yelled: "Jay run – run Jay!" A tree he was cutting down for firewood was about to land on top of me. Unable to avoid the falling tree, I was knocked into a state of semi-unconsciousness. We still laugh and reminisce about the tree falling on me.

WETHERINGTON - ROBINSON ELEMENTARY

My childhood memories of my most embarrassing and humiliating moments remain vivid today. Three negative experiences involved being arrested for shop lifting a miniature hot-wheel car out of Roses Department Store; getting a part of my anatomy stuck in my zipper and having to go to emergency room; and receiving several beatings from a teacher and principal. I was paddled by the school principal, Mr. Horn for tearing up tiny pieces of paper while standing in line at a school assembly.

My third grade teacher, Ms. Butler, bless her soul, beat me with a fan belt for running after a ball that crossed the bus route. Ms. Butler was a great teacher and I believe she sparked something in me which was inspiring. It was at this age that I begin to read voraciously. She chose me to sing "White Christmas" in the School's Christmas Assembly Program. She played the piano and practiced the song several times with me. This was the first time at school that I received any positive recognition. Ms. Butler recognized there was something about me which was worth cultivating. Not only did I sing the song before the entire student assembly, but she made me memorize the words which I still recall today.

Chapter Six

BUSTED!

Thou shall not steal. Exodus 20:15 KJV

Going into Valdosta to shop for groceries and clothing was one of my most memorable experiences as a young boy. We did not make it into town too often and it required finding someone to give us a ride there and back. This was usually accomplished through a neighbor name Mr. RJ or Mr. Lawrence as they were one of the few black families who actually owned an automobile. Often times, my mother would send me to their homes to ask them for a ride into town. They were always nice and seemed happy to accommodate us. Madear would always give them money for gas.

On one particular occasion, my mother and I had gone into town to the Five Points Shopping Center where there were a host of stores which included Roses Department Store. I decided to wander off from my mother and look at some merchandise. I was drawn to a miniature car, a Mattel's product known as a "Hot-wheel." I just knew my mother could not afford to buy this toy for me and I wasn't about to ask her to do so. Yet, I was allured by its bright shiny red finish and thought it would be pleasing for play.

I decided to put it in my pocket and ease out of the store without anyone knowing I had taken it. Little did I know that security was observing. As soon as I made it out of the store, I was busted and brought back in the store. My heart stopped when I realized I had been caught and now faced the biggest problem of my young life. Tears began to roll down my cheeks and I knew what I had done was wrong. I would do anything to undo what had just occurred. I was having the worst day of my life and all I could think about was the punishment that I would surely receive when grandfather found out about my mischief.

While sitting in the store security office, I wandered where my mother was and if she would come and get me. Moments later, two uniform officers from the Valdosta Police Department showed up and escorted me out of the store and put me in the back of their cruiser. I was on my way to jail and my heart started pounding faster as tears continued to roll down my cheeks. All I could think about was what had I done and how was I going to get out of all of this trouble.

The officers seemed nice enough, and engaged me in some small talk. I'm sure this was probably a common occurrence for them but one which I hoped to never experience again. My mother had no idea what had happened to me as she was still shopping and did not know I had been arrested.

After what seemed like an eternity of waiting at the station, my neighbor and our landlord, Ms. Bay, picked me up from the police station. I was so happy to be leaving the police station but knew what was waiting for me when I arrived at home. I just knew that Grandfather was going to "tan my hide" for stealing.

Upon arriving home, everything was peaceful. I don't remember much about what was said, if anything was said at all. Amazingly, my grandfather did not lay one hand on me. I believe it was because my grandmother probably told him I had been through enough and not to punish me. I don't know what happened, but I was thankful to avoid a severe thrashing. What seemed to be the worst day of my, life did not end up so bad after all. Nevertheless, I understood that I still had to go before a judge. I learned my lesson, "Thou shalt not steal." Exodus 20:15 KJV

Several weeks later, I appeared in the judge's chamber with my mother. I have no recollection of who the judge was or what he said to my mother and me. Many years later, after submitting my application to become an attorney in the State of Florida, I was required to report any arrest as an adult or juvenile and provide the records of same. Upon inquiry with the clerk of court for Lowndes County, Georgia, there was no record of my detention or juvenile record.

While most of my friends in middle-school decided to participate in sports, I opted to become a member of the band. My sister, Helen, left her clarinet at the house when she moved to Lansing, Michigan to live with Aunt Liz and finish her senior year of high school. My junior high-school band director, Mr. Bobby Godwin, is an excellent clarinet player. We continue to stay in touch as Facebook friends. I am grateful for his tutelage and musical training which assisted me in pursuing a college education. I decided that if I was going to be a member of the band, I needed to play a manly instrument. Consequently, this led me to switch instruments from the clarinet to the bass horn also known as a tuba or sousaphone. Little did I know that by switching instruments, I would be recruited to play in the esteemed college band known then as the "Marching Men of Cookman" now called "the Marching Wildcats" of Bethune - Cookman University.

My last paddling occurred while at Lowndes County Jr. High. I thought that skipping my English Class and going to play basketball in the gym was a good idea. This was a terrible error in judgment that had profound consequences. While sitting in the band class, I was advised to report to Mr. Jesse Clark, the Industrial Arts teacher. He told me I would have to receive three pounds for skipping class. I submitted without any protest. Those three lightning strikes changed my life forever. My derriere was set on fire and I had only received one lick which caused my knees to buckle. I was not sure I could sustain another blow from Mr. Clark. The sound of the board striking my rear end seemed to resonate throughout the entire school. He did not hesitate to strike again and I experienced numbness and burning bringing water to my eyes. The third strike from Mr. Clark sealed the deal. Thanks to Mr. Clark, I would never skip class again.

Fortunately for me, there were other male figures around me who had admirable personal attributes. It was the characteristics of many people who I met along my life's journey that helped me reach my full potential.

Uncle J.V., my father's brother, was a character among characters and he loved to tease you and stir up commotion with everyone. He had a great work ethic but he loved his libations. Uncle J.V. took an interest in me and would often take me fishing when I visited him and Aunt Liz during summer breaks in Lansing, Michigan. Although my mother and father were never married, Aunt Liz is my mother's sister and Uncle J.V. was my father's brother. It seemed only natural that my aunt and uncle would treat me like their own child at Christmas because of the familial relationship. I regret not being able to attend Uncle J.V.'s funeral as I was in college when he died and could not afford to travel to Michigan. I will always remember his kindness and goodness toward me. "What you say thar boy?" was one of his favorite expressions as he would bellow it with a disguised animated voice through his nostrils.

Over indulgence in libations was a common occurrence among some of my uncles. It was not uncommon for some of them to rise early on a Sunday morning and go to the "Shine House" to purchase bootleg liquor or "moonshine." On one occasion, Uncle Leroy and Uncle Eugene (Luke) were struck by a train while on their way home from an early morning venture of drinking. The train took off the rear bed of Uncle Leroy's pickup truck. With the exception of some soiled pants, they both arrived home without a scratch. When my uncles were sober, they were hard working men. I loved being around them and learned many things.

As some of them grew older, they stopped drinking and committed their lives to serving God. Master Leroy Wright was one of my favorite uncles. We moved next door to Uncle Leroy and Aunt Lillar, my mother's sister, when I was in middle school. Uncle Leroy had dark ebony skin, and a diminutive muscular build with the strength of an ox. I loved playing checkers with him and arm wrestling. He would always let me borrow his pickup truck if I needed to go somewhere. He married my mother's sister, Lillar Mae (Aunt Lil), and they had eight children. Their son, Amos and I were a few years apart but we spent a lot of time together working in the fields and playing sandlot football with our neighbors on weekends.

Affectionately called "Da" by his children and grandchildren, Uncle Leroy was a school bus driver and foreman for the Valdosta Chief of Police's tobacco farm. Uncle Leroy, much like Uncle J.V., loved to tease you and if you did not have a tough skin when you met him, you would have one afterwards. Uncle Leroy was a father-figure to me and he always kept everybody laughing and working.

His favorite saying to a worker was, "I'm going to dot you!" This meant he was going to pay you less for not working as you should. This was done in jest to the worker and it created levity while we were working. Without Uncle Leroy's help, I would not have been able to get my driver's license when I turned sixteen. He allowed me to drive his Chevy pickup truck to Georgia License Division and use it to take the driving test. It was in the tobacco field with Uncle Leroy that I first learned to drive a tractor. While cropping tobacco (picking the ripen leaves from the stalk) the workers would often rush to finish their rows in order to drive the tractor.

I spent many days with Uncle Leroy, Aunt Lil and their crew of workers laboring in the tobacco fields under the blazing South Georgia heat. They taught me to work hard and do your job well. Hard work has never killed anyone; it only makes you stronger and a better person. Field work is hard but it built character. More importantly, it inspired me toward a career with a more conducive work environment.

Chapter Seven

The Field

Work ethic

The best gift I received from my family was having a good work ethic. At the age of ten, I began working as a tobacco handler. Before the age of technology in the tobacco industry, the crop was harvested with field hands known as croppers. Their task was to go into the field and collect the ripened leaves of tobacco from the stalks and place it in sleds which were pulled by tractors. The sleds would deliver the leaves to a barn where normally women would be busily sewing the tobacco on sticks that men would hang in the barn to cure.

The stringer would receive the tobacco leaves from several handlers on each side. My first job was handing tobacco to the sewer who would then string the leaves on a stick that would be placed into the barn for curation. It would usually take about half a day to gather the crop for our neighbor and employer, Mr. Julian Johnson. Mr. Johnson was a very soft spoken and kind hearted white man who lived less than a half a mile up the road from us. He never failed to bring my grandparents a box of oranges at Christmas time. I would earn $5.00 for working a half day. Mr. Johnson would always pay us with brand new $5.00 bills.

Every year, I saved almost every dollar I made until the end of the summer and used it to buy clothes and supplies for school. Everyone in my household would also work for Mr. Johnson. Grandfather would unload the sleds and stack the tobacco so high that the handlers could barely see over the stack leaves. My mother, grandmother, and sisters would work at the barns. I envied the field croppers and yearned to join them as this is where the young and older men worked.

Eventually, I would become a cropper and spend many summer days in the wet cool mornings and blazing South Georgia sun cropping tobacco. Often times the water which collected on the plants would invade my eyes and bring about a stinging effect which temporarily blurred my vision. The tar from the tobacco would also cause the hair on my arm to curl up into balls. Much scrubbing and washing was required to free the tar from your body after a long hard day of work.

Cropping tobacco required bending over at the waist to reach down to the bottom of the stalk and only remove the leaves which were ripe for picking. By the end of the day, you would definitely feel the pain in your back from being in that position for several hours. It helped to have long arms as it allowed me to collect a large load of leaves before walking to place them in a sled. There was always competition among the croppers to finish your row first. The rows were normally in lines of four with a pathway between them for the tractor and sled.

The rows seemed endless in some fields. I worked in the tobacco fields every summer until I was able to find other employment. The hard work built character and helped me realized that I did not want to spend my life working in a tobacco field. Working in fields made me appreciate the value of a dollar and the importance of being frugal. I also learned the importance of doing your job well even when no one was watching you. The characteristic of integrity is a vital part of the recipe for success in any endeavor. It is often defined as what you do when no one is watching.

Working in tobacco required you to get up early in the morning, ride on the back of a pickup truck in the coolness of the early morning and go into a field of tobacco which was wet and grassy. Your clothing would be soaked until the heat of the day would cause them to dry. The temperature would sear to 100 degrees or greater. We would take about an hour for a lunch break and return to the field to finish out the work day. The favorite time of the day was receiving your pay which was always in the form of cash. The pay for a day of labor rose from about $10 a day to around $60 a day by the time I performed my last day of labor in the tobacco field.

Eventually, I saved up enough money to buy my first car from working in the tobacco fields. My brother-in law, Shorty, sold me his 1964 Pontiac Catalina for $400. This was one of the proudest moments in my life. I spent many Saturday mornings cropping tobacco for Shorty and his father, Mr. Gay Wright. As a result of my hard work, I purchased my first car in my junior year of high school.

The gift of a strong work ethic would carry me much further than any talent that I possessed. That trait would also inspire one of my close high school friends on to success as well. The most important qualities that you can instill in a child are manners, respect and the willingness to work hard. That strong work ethic is what would take me from the field to the court.

Once a task has begun,

never leave it till it's done.

Be the labor, large or small, do it well or not at all.

Author Unknown

James Pierce 76

Chapter Eight

Race Relations

On the evening May 16, 1918, in Lowndes County, Georgia Sydney Johnson, a young 18 year old black man, shot and killed 25-year old white plantation owner Hampton Smith. Smith was known to abuse and beat his black workers. His reputation for cruelty and harshness toward black workers made recruiting workers so difficult that he had to use convict labor. Smith paid Sidney Johnson's $30 fine for playing dice and forced him to work on his plantation. Johnson sustained several beatings from Smith. Johnson had been ruthlessly beaten by Smith for refusing to work while he was sick.

Sidney Johnson was apprehended several days later during a shootout in Valdosta. Following his death, a crowd of over 700, castrated him and dragged his body down Patterson Street. Following the violence, African Americans fled from Lowndes County and Brooks County in fear of losing their lives. The lynching spree of May 1918 in Lowndes County was part of a large trend of organized violence towards African Americans after War World One. By 1922 local chapters of the Ku Klux Klan were holding rallies openly in Valdosta and throughout the southern states. I know my grandparents were fearful about what was occurring not only in Valdosta, but throughout the South.

Johnson's pregnant wife, Mary Turner, denied that her husband had been involved in Smith's killing and publicly opposed her husband's murder. She threatened to have members of the mob arrested causing the mob to focus on her. She fled when she learned of the mob's intent, but was captured and taken to Folsom Bridge over the Little River which separates Brooks and Lowndes Counties. After the mob tied her ankles and hung her upside down from a tree, she was doused with gasoline and motor oil and burned alive.

While Mary was still alive, a member of the mob split her abdomen open with a knife. Her baby fell on the ground where it was stomped and crushed after giving a cry. Turner's body was pierced with hundreds of bullets. Mary Turner and her child were buried at the site of the lynching and a whiskey bottle was used to mark the grave.

From May 17 to May 24, 1918, thirteen African Americans, including pregnant twenty-one year old Mary Turner, were lynched. This scene of racial violence is documented in the Black and White Wax Museum located in Baltimore, Maryland and it was there that I first learned of this horrific incident.

I can only imagine the fear and anxiety which my grandparents experienced as a young married couple when these events transpired. Despite the atrocities which were occurring all around them, they persevered and raised their children in this place which I call my hometown.

At the time, Georgia governor Hugh Dorsey was given a complete investigation of the murders which included the names of two instigators and 15 participants. No one was ever arrested, or charged for the vigilante murders. A historical marker memorializing Turner was placed near the lynching site and was dedicated on May 15, 2010. In July of 2013, the marker was found to have been riddled with five bullet holes by an unknown vandal.

My first encounter with racial prejudice occurred when I was a young child. There were a group of white field workers who would routinely pass by our home and throw bottles and other objects at me while I was playing or standing in our front yard. I had no idea what provoked their behavior, and fortunately I was never struck or injured by their missiles. The first white people I actually met were very amiable and often generous toward our family.

The Stubbs lived about a mile or less down the road from us in a beautiful wooden southern styled home which still stands today. It was on this property where we would go on Saturday mornings to gather the tobacco crops for Mr. Johnson. Mrs. Stubbs and Mr. Johnson would eventually get married. Mrs. Stubbs had three children from her previous marriage, Joe, Ann, and Lee. Every Christmas, Mr. and Mrs. Johnson would give out boxes of oranges to the families that helped them on the farm. The Stubbs children were always respectful and like their parents were just kind and lovable people.

After completing the 6th Grade at Wetherington-Robinson Elementary, I attended Lowndes Jr. High School. My first year as a Golden Eagle (school mascot) was fairly uneventful with the exception of entering a desegregated school after completing my first six years of education in a segregated school. One must ponder why did it take so long as The United States Supreme Court declared that "separate was not equal" in the 1954 case of Brown v. Board of Education of Topeka.

Desegregation in Lowndes County did not begin until 1966. Lowndes County Schools disregarded the ruling of the United States Supreme Court and carried on business as usual. In December of 1967 a hearing examiner for the Department of Health Education and Welfare (HEW), recommended a $342,000 cut in federal funds to Lowndes County Schools for non-compliance with the Civil Rights Act of 1964.

In July of 1968, Lowndes County remained non-compliant with the guidelines of HEW, and as a result received a $480,000 cut in federal funds in its school budget. On July 11, 1968, Lowndes County and several other Georgia Counties were sued by the Justice Department for failure to eliminate their dual school systems. The Superintendent and fellow board members were named defendants in the case.

The charges against them included unfair employment and appointment of teachers based on race, a sub-standard curriculum in black schools, and a bus system devised to prevent desegregation and several other violations of the Civil Rights. The Superintendent and the other five defendants were found guilty of violating the 1964 Civil

Rights Act and given 60 days to come up with a desegregation plan that complied with the HEW requirements. Alternatively, the Court would implement its own desegregation plan.

The Lowndes Board of Education decided to consolidate eight all white schools and four all black schools that were operating in the county. The Board decided to close the four black schools and expand the predominately white schools. There was some controversy over the closing of all the predominantly black schools; some members of the black community felt it was unfair for all the black children to be forced into white schools.

The Board presented its plan for desegregation to Judge Bootle who accepted it eventually with the conditions that it would be completed by September 1970. However, the Justice Department was not satisfied with Lowndes desegregation plan. The Justice Department agreed to accept the plan provided two changes were made. First, all seniors at Westside High, a predominately black school, had to be transferred to Lowndes High. Secondly, the number of faculty crossovers for the 1969-1970 school year had to be delineated.

Lowndes approved the movement of the students at Westside High and recommended a five to one ratio of white to black teachers in each school. Although the county met its ratio, the movement of faculty had a greater impact on African American teachers.

According to Dr. Shirley Hardin, Valdosta State University (VSU) Director of African American Studies, African American teachers were more likely to receive demotions when they were transferred to new schools. Many African American high school teachers became middle or even elementary school teachers in the integrated schools. Appointment of principals and other administrative positions were controversial issues.

The band director for the Westside High Marching braves, Mr. Samuel C. Berry, became an assistant director under Billy Martin at Lowndes County. Mr. Berry, a graduate of Florida A & M University and former member of the famous Marching 100 Rattler Band, had established an excellent Marching Band at Westside High.

Marching Men *Of* Cookman

SAMUEL C. BERRY DIRECTOR OF BANDS BETHUNE – COOKMAN COLLEGE

My sister, Helen, played the clarinet in the Westside High marching band. My cousin, Wallace Johnson, and neighbor, Kenneth Haynes, played trumpet in the Westside High marching band. Wallace, a diminutive trumpet player, would bring the half-time crowd to their feet as a soloist when the band played "Grazing in the Grass." I would later use my sister's clarinet as my own to participate in the beginning band program at Lowndes Jr. High. I would later join Kenny Haynes as a member of the "Marching Men of Cookman."

Lowndes High School first opened its doors in the fall of 1966. The new school was the result of the consolidation of two former rivals, Hahira High School and Lowndes County High School. 1966 was also the first year of real integration in Lowndes County. Westside High School consolidated with Lowndes High in the Fall of 1969. Despite the controversy and opposition to integration, the 1969-year went by without major conflict and I found myself attending school with white classmates for the first time in 1970.

It was a positive experience for me and many African Americans. Nevertheless, everything was not flawless. White members of Lowndes High girls' basketball team refused to share a room with their African American teammates. Despite that episode and long delay, desegregation in Lowndes County was peaceful and was accomplished without any violent repercussions.

Chapter Nine

Marching

In fall of 1973, I attended my first high-school band camp at Lowndes High school which is still located on St. Augustine Road and can be seen from Interstate 75. The Lowndes County Marching Viking band like many high-school bands used a drum and bugle corps style marching step. This marching style is more like walking rather than high step marching which is prevalent in the historical black college and university bands. The corps styled required considerable less effort to play and perform routines especially if you are carrying a tuba which weighs about 25 to 50 pounds depending on whether it was made from fiberglass or metal.

As a member of the high-school marching and concert band, I was able to travel to many places and cities for competition and football games. I would have never gone to Niagara Falls, New York and Canada but for participating in the Greatest Band in North America Competition, which our band won during my junior year. It was in band that I made several lifelong friends and even attended Bethune-Cookman College now Bethune-Cookman University with another classmate and trumpet player, Donald Jenkins. Donald, or DJ as we called him, is now the Director of Bands for Robert E. Lee High-School in Jacksonville, Florida.

In high-school, Donald and I along with several other members would get together and have jam sessions. We called our group of African American musicians the "Soul Patrol." We wanted to play our brand of music which was "Funk" and "Rhythm and Blues." Our band director, Mr. Martin, who we called "Billy Slick" recognized our need and desire to play what we called "soul music." Consequently, he allowed us to perform our music while in the stands during the football games. The fans would get excited when Donald, Harry, and Martinez would play the fanfare from Kool & the Gang's "Hollywood Swinging" and I would blast the bass line from the Ohio Player's "Skin Tight" or we would play the theme from the popular dance show, *Soul Train*.

My experience in high school band helped me to develop character and discipline. Unlike many high school and college bands, we were required to memorize our music for marching band performances. This required a certain amount of individual practice and lugging my Tuba home and bringing it back on the school bus until I purchased my car. Some of the students would make fun of me bringing a tuba on the bus but I did not care about what they said. We spent many hours on the practice field and in the band room rehearsing our music. We would also have car washes on weekends and various fundraisers during the school year for expenses in order to attend marching band competitions.

Mr. Martin was an excellent trumpet player and motivator. We would always perform a chant at the end of each marching band practice session which went as follows:

H – honor!

U- unity!

S-superior!

T-teamwork!

L-leadership!

E- effort

What do we have? Hustle!

We had a tremendous amount of pride in our high school band and expected to win all of our marching band competitions. Superior ratings were always the goal in our competitions and there are numerous trophies displayed representing the success of the Marching Vikings now known as the Bridge-men throughout the school's existence.

Lowndes High School Marching Band 1974

Fortunately, on one occasion, Mr. Berry bought the Marching Men of Cookman to Martin Stadium and put on a performance just for our band. Immediately, Donald and I knew that we wanted to be a part of this high stepping, dancing and playing, swinging and swaying historical black college band known as "The Marching Men of Cookman." Several former band members from Westside High School and Lowndes County High School had attended the Bethune-Cookman and marched in the band under Dr. Samuel C. Berry.

Donald and I along with many other band freshmen from throughout the country would find that becoming a member of the Marching Men of Cookman was no easy task and we would have to earn our way into this esteemed organization through much toil, hard work, sweat and even tears for many.

During our junior year in high-school, both Donald, Harry, and I tried out for the two drum major positions. Neither one of us made it, but Donald and I were section leaders of our instrument group during our senior year and we both were soloist during the half-time performances. Donald could rip a high C which is an amazing feat for a trumpet player. We became great friends and even went on double dates on a few occasions.

JAMES PIERCE, DONALD JENKINS, WANDA (WRIGHT) TODD,

In the summer of 1976, I worked in a steel mill making grills and bumpers for automobiles to save money for college. This was a high risk operation and required me to operate heavy metal cutting machinery while wearing lines attached to your hands to make sure they did not get severed by the machines. This was hard and dangerous work for anyone, but I was just happy to have a full time job that was not out in a tobacco field.

I would later sell my 1964 Pontiac Catalina for $50 after the engine blew leaving a cloud of smoke behind me. Even if the engine had not blown, I could not afford to keep my car. It leaked about a quart of oil every day. I was buying oil by the case to keep it running and it was not feasible to take it to college.

After graduating from high school, I chose to take a different route than that of going north to work in the automobile industry. I decided to attend a private college founded by Dr. Mary McCleod Bethune, the child of former slaves whom scraped together $1.50 to begin a school with five African American girls in 1904. After a tumultuous beginning, her unshakable faith and remarkable organizational skills transformed the Literary and Industrial School for Training Negro Girls, to a high school, junior college, and Bethune-Cookman University.

Dr. Bethune was the adviser to four presidents, a brilliant speaker, astute fundraiser, and defied the Klu Klux Klan. She provided money to pay the poll tax and lead African American voters to the polls. Dr. Bethune embodied intelligence and courage during times of hostility, intimidation and violence against blacks. She stated the following about starting her school:

"I had no furniture. I begged dry goods boxes and made benches and stools, begged a basin and other things I needed and in 1904 five little girls here started school." Dr. Mary Mcleod Bethune 1875 -1955.

Dr. Mary McCloud Bethune was a true visionary. Without her vision of starting a school, Bethune-Cookman University would not exist and I would not be telling you my story. One of the most important ingredients for success in life is having the power of vision. I firmly believe that whatever you can conceive, and believe you can achieve. It's like a great golf shot; you must see it, feel it, trust it, and execute it.

Your vision determines how far or not you will go in your life. You must expect your vision will happen and assume full responsibility for obtaining it regardless of the difficult circumstances you must overcome. It is written, "Without vision, the people perish" (Proverbs 29:18 King James Version). Ghandi wisely proclaimed: "A man is but the product of his thoughts. What he thinks he becomes."

MARCHING MEN OF COOKMAN

Chapter Ten

COLLEGE LIFE

In 1969, Bethune Cookman's President Richard V. Moore hired Dr. Samuel C. Berry as the director of bands at Bethune-Cookman College. His mission was to develop an exciting music program. The marching band quickly gained notoriety and became known as the marching and playing, swinging and swaying, Marching Men of Cookman. During the next ten years Samuel Berry created and perfected a sound and style of performance that laid the groundwork for what is today the Marching Wildcats of Bethune-Cookman University (The Pride). His dynamic leadership and professional creativity allowed the Marching Men of B-CC to become a household name in college band circles. He passed away in 1980 and was inducted posthumously into the Bethune-Cookman University Hall of fame in 2012.

Dr. Berry, often referred to as "Red Dog" because of his red complexion and membership in the Omega Psi Phi Fraternity, was the consummate professional. As noted by many former members of the band, I would not be where I am today but for the leadership, work ethic, and professionalism demanded by Dr. Berry. *Alba Berry, Widow of Samuel Berry remarked at his induction to the BCU Hall of fame:*

"Every time the B-CU band performs is a tribute to Berry, the former Bethune-Cookman band director who laid the ground work for what is today's edition of the Marching Wildcats. That bold sound emanates from the work Samuel did," said Mrs. Berry.

Dr. Larry Handfield, former Bethune –Cookman Drum Major, prominent South Florida attorney, former Trustee Chairperson at B-CU and a major contributor to the University also paid tribute to Dr. Samuel C. Berry: "If it weren't for Samuel Berry, I wouldn't be here," Handfield said.

As Donald (DJ) boarded the Greyhound bus with our trunks packed with all of our material possessions, we had no idea what we would encounter upon arriving at Bethune-Cookman College. As section leaders, DJ for the trumpets and I for the bass horns, we were confident in our abilities as musicians and leaders.

Like most organizations on traditional historically black colleges and universities, hazing freshman band members was a long standing tradition of the Marching Men of Cookman. Hazing may be defined as a process based on a tradition that is used by groups to discipline and to maintain a hierarchy. In the band, the freshmen were referred to as crabs and the upper classmen were our big brothers. The freshmen were considered to be thralls to the big brothers and were expected to answer to their every request. Regardless of consent, the rituals require individuals to engage in activities that are physically and psychologically stressful. Those freshmen who resisted were said to have an attitude and would usually be singled out for greater harassment.

These activities can be humiliating, demeaning, intimidating, and exhausting, all of which results in physical and/or emotional discomfort. Hazing is about group dynamics and proving one's worthiness to become a member of the specific group. My first memory of arriving at B-CC was being asked to get down on the ground and perform push-ups for some big brothers.

Every day of freshman band camp involved waking up and being in line to perform calisthenics at 5:30 a.m. These exercises had me and my brothers in the best shape of our entire lives. Then the freshman would form two lines and march across the campus singing a traditional freshman song:

Aww BC, Aww BC Wildcats! Give me some slack, Cause if you don't – I want -scratch your back! But if you do, I swear – I'll march for you! The Marching Men! (hands clapping) CLAP! CLAP!CLAP!CLAP! (pause) CLAP! CLAP!CLAP!CLAP! Are Coming In! CLAP! CLAP!CLAP!CLAP! CLAP! CLAP!CLAP!CLAP! We got Soul! CLAP! CLAP!CLAP!CLAP! CLAP! CLAP!CLAP!CLAP! So let's Go! CLAP! CLAP!CLAP!CLAP! CLAP! CLAP!CLAP!CLAP!

We marched and sung everyday on our way to breakfast, lunch, and dinner. Once we had our meal, we would line up outside the cafeteria in the area known as "The Quad." We would then greet all the big brothers by calling their names out in unison. Good morning Big Brother COOOL Freddy! Good morning Big Brother Mean Jean! Good morning Big Brother Dean Portier! This would go on until we had recognized every big brother who was present.

Each freshman was given a band name. I was called Apache, and DJ was called Pretty Paula. Our other roommate, Rufus was called Bugus. Both of my college roommates would go on to earn degrees in Music Education and become band directors. Rufus Redding was band director for Jones High School and was responsible for sending many musicians to play in the band at Bethune-Cookman. Donald Jenkins is currently the band director for Robert E. Lee High School in Jacksonville, Florida.

Some other freshman names included, Tampon and Crowbar from Leesburg, Florida. Then there were my fellow freshmen tuba player brothers, Mustank, and Mary Hartman. Koombus, Tweety Bird and Soultrain were from Miami and there were many more names given to the freshman such as Lemon Head, Sugar Bear, Peanut and Nub. Nub played the baritone with one hand. Even today, many of us are still known only by our freshman band names.

Unfortunately for me, I was harassed more than any other freshman. This was partly due to my ineptness in learning the dance routines and various maneuvers with my instrument. Twirling a tuba was not an easy thing to do. We had many motions with our instruments which were all done in sequential order. It was a fascinating performance to watch as the movements would start at the beginning of the line and smoothly flow repetitiously to the end. There was a learning curve that I had to overcome. It was made more difficult when you were being scolded for making an error and made to do pushups or run around the field with a tuba over your head. The Tuba section, known as the "Terror Ten" was one of the premier sections of band because of our showmanship in twirling our large instruments. I was disappointed when I did not march in the first football game half-time show.

There were nine upperclassmen in the tuba section and only one position that needed to be filled. Roderick Carter (Mustank) earned the last position. He was definitely more ready than me and although I wanted to be on the field, Mustank was better and deserved to be there. After missing that game, I played in every half-time performance until I decided to leave the band.

One day a big brother, who we called Arrowhead, told me to do a rain dance. It did not seem like an unreasonable request. However, I did such a good job that whenever any big brother would stop me, they would order me to do my rain dance. Of course I complied because I did not want to refuse and get a reputation for having an attitude. Many times I would get stopped in the cafeteria or my way to class and ordered to do my rain dance. At first it was not a big deal and it was better than doing pushups. As each day went by, it became more embarrassing and humiliating. I was determined not to give up. I would just do that stupid rain dance and move forward.

Becoming a member of the Marching Men of Cookman was one the most difficult challenges I would face in my entire life. We practiced our instrument movements and dance routines daily along with a high stepping march that required you to strike a 90 degree angle with your toes pointed straight to the ground and your knee and hip extended to waist level. This style of marching was physically demanding and unlike the corp style marching technique we performed at Lowndes High School. Additionally, we had to learn to play our instruments while performing a dance routine during each half-time show.

Learning the dance routine was difficult for me. The harassment from the big brothers did not make it any easier. Mustank and I were the only freshman tuba players to make it out of four that showed up for freshman band camp. While Mustank easily learned the various routines, I struggled to master the routines.

Unfortunately, every time I would make a mistake, we both would have to do push- ups. I felt bad for Mustank. I made so many mistakes that they got tired of punishing me, and would punish him. Mustank was from Lake City which was less than 60 miles from my hometown. He was an excellent musician and quick learner. He also had an older brother, Lynwood, who was a senior and played the baritone.

Mustank and I remain great friends today and I have great respect for him. He would become a member of the Morrocan Sheiks Band at Bush Gardens where he played the trombone. The renown Sheiks would travel worldwide and was a feature entertainment act for many years at Busch Gardens.

There were certain big brothers who tended to harass you more. One of the most intimidating big brothers was a member of our tuba section. We knew him as Big Brother "Booga Bear." He stood about 6'3' and had a corpulent figure. He was quite intimidating for every freshman who experienced his wrath. He loved to strike Mustank and I on our elbows with the tuba mouth piece. Our elbows would be tender not only from making popping sounds with the inner portion of our elbow on our instruments but also from Booga Bear striking them with his mouth piece. He would make the freshman find him cigarettes. On one occasion, Booga Bear decided to thrash us with a belt for something I probably did wrong during a half time show. He just loved to make our life and other band freshmen's lives miserable.

Being out on the practice field during the blazing Florida sun was mentally and physically exhausting. Our section leaders, Roderick Florence (Kaboobie) and Fortune Bell (TP), were great leaders and hard workers. They held all the members of our section responsible for performing with excellence.

During band camp, we would practice 12 or more hours a day. As freshmen, Mustank and I had to make sure all of the upperclassmen instruments in our section were carried to the field for them. We would have our sectional practices in the morning and evening during summer band camp. Those would normally be followed by a full marching practice after the practice inside the band room. We were greatly relieved when school started as it cut down the number of practices and opportunities for harassment by the big brothers.

As band freshmen, we were expected to adhere to certain unwritten rules. A few of them included no sweets; no talking to females; and no walking on the grass or wearing school colors. We were also expected to wear our white Tee shirts with our freshman names on the back and short pants during band rehearsals.

On one evening during sectional rehearsal, I felt the need to stand up and confront the big brothers after I had been struck in the chest. I threw a kick into the chest of Big Brother Dawg and assumed a fighting stance. Knowing I did not have a chance of winning a fight with them, I fled the band room and went to my room vowing that I would not return to suffer more harassment. Basically, I was fed up with being abused and was willing to give up and go back home.

Fortunately, my roommates and Mustank talked me into returning to practice the next day. If I had given up, I probably would have spent the rest of my life in Valdosta and not gone back to college. As expected, my return yielded even more harassment but it seemed like the big brothers had a little more respect for me because they knew I would fight if pushed to my limits.

Our plight as band freshmen continued for the entire football season. Often times the band freshmen in previous years were allowed to "go over" during the regular season. This meant you were now no longer required to answer to the big brothers and follow the freshmen rules. We did not make it over until the last game of the season, which always is against our arch rival, Florida A&M University Rattlers.

Going over and becoming full fledge members of the Marching Men of Cookman was one of the most memorable moments in my life and in the lives of my freshmen band brothers. We all immediately rushed to the college book store to purchase our Marching Men of Cookman shirts. This was the proudest moment of our lives. Being recognized as a Marching Man on campus gave us instant respect by the student body and a sense of pride for an organization that we had never experienced. We were now fully fledged band brothers in the Marching Men of Cookman!

Terror Ten

RUFUS REDDING (FORMER BAND DIRECTOR JONES HIGH SCHOOL)
JAMES PIERCE AND RODERICK CARTER

Terror Ten

Terror Ten

Charles Florence, Sr.

Chapter Eleven

ACADEMIC EXCELLENCE

Throughout my later elementary grades, middle school and high school, I managed to make decent grades and barely missed graduating with honors in high school. The notion of academic excellence was thrust to the forefront of my consciousness by Dr. Oswald P. Bronson. Dr. Bronson served as President of Bethune-Cookman College for 29 years. He served not only as an effective leader, but as a role model for anyone seeking to understand how to conduct one's professional and personal life in an ethical and compassionate manner. He coined the greeting, "My friends" as his way of addressing the student body. Dr. Bronson spent sixteen years as a pastor in churches in Florida, Georgia and Illinois prior to his career in academia and higher education. In 1975 while serving as President of the Interdenominational Theological Center in Atlanta, he was selected by Bethune-Cookman College to be its president. He held that position until 2004. His leadership, wisdom and appreciation for each individual are entrenched in his faith and beliefs.

Dr. Bronson's biography, *Chief Servant*, provides great insight of his philosophy for life and approach to leadership. Bethune Cookman's motto, "Enter to learn, depart to serve," definitely was part of the genesis which guided his life. Dr. Bronson set forth the following gem of thought on academic excellence in his memoirs, *Living a Life of Gratitude*.

"In all that you do, pursue excellence. Excellence is a commitment to academic integrity. Excellence means rising above the ordinary and engaging in superior performance. Excellence is in both the thinking and the doing."

This powerful lesson for life motivated me to strive for excellence in all my endeavors. I worked hard to get good grades, went to class regularly and made the Dean's list every semester. I enjoyed college life, concerts and the fraternity parties immensely. But I learned to balance fun and recreation with academic work. Self-discipline is important not only in school but in one's occupation and life. As a student, self-discipline made me come home at an appropriate time so I could make it to class on time and fulfill my academic obligations.

I am extremely thankful to Dr. Bronson for his inspiration and major accomplishments as our "Chief Servant" of Bethune- Cookman College. Several years ago, I had the pleasure of taking Dr. Bronson to lunch and he was extremely proud of my accomplishments as a Bethune-Cookman Graduate. Dr. and Mrs. Bronson represent the utopia marital relationship and are extremely warm and caring people. Those qualities are also found in his children. I am proud to be among Dr. Bronson's first graduating class in 1980 that was under his complete leadership for four years. I received my Bachelor Arts Degree in Political Science with Magna Cum Laude honors.

Upon arriving at Bethune-Cookman, both DJ and I had planned to become band directors. As with most colleges and universities, the first year is primarily basic courses which are unrelated to your specific field of study. Several months later, I knew that I did not want to major in music and become a band director. I considered majoring in history but this offered little for prospective employment and I was more interested in current events. While reviewing the curriculum of possible majors, I stumbled upon Political Science. While I figured it had something to do with politics, I was not sure what the major entailed.

I decided to visit the Political Science department chairperson, Dr. Jake Miller. Dr. Miller was very soft spoken and little did I know, he would be one of my greatest mentors and supporters throughout my life. He encouraged me to write and continue my pursuit of becoming a judge when I had placed those aspirations on the back burner.

Dr. Miller nurtured and prepared me for law school. He was directly responsible for helping me obtain a full tuition scholarship to Stetson University College of Law so long as I maintained certain academic standards and assisted with minority recruitment. He was also directly responsible for many other students obtaining financial support to attend post graduate school. Dr. Miller, a former marine, and brother of Alpha Phi Alpha Fraternity, Incorporated was a godly man who graduated from Bethune - Cookman College with a B.S. in 1951. He received his Master's Degree from the University of Illinois in 1957 and PH.D in Political Science from the University of North Carolina at Chapel Hill in 1967.

His lifelong interest in international affairs is reflected in his travel, teaching and writing. He directed summer study programs to West Africa and the Caribbean and conducted research in West Africa, Ethiopia and Haiti. He authored three books, *The Black Presence in Foreign Affairs* (1978), *The Plight of Haitian Refugees* (1984), and *Bethune-Cookman College and Beyond* (1996). He also published numerous articles and papers. Through his writing and public speeches, he argued the causes of the hungry, the homeless and refugees. His post-retirement publications included a book of poetry entitled, *Building a Better World* (1996).

His warm and loving demeanor touched many lives and precious memories were made by those who encountered him along his journey. His smile was contagious and the words he often shared with me and others were full of great wisdom and sage advice. He was a catalyst and force pushing each generation to fulfill their dreams using education as the foundation to their successes. He spent endless hours grading term papers and reviewing them with me and other students to help improve our analytical and writing skills.

He truly cared about every student and went beyond the call of duty to not only prepare them for graduate school but also assist them with financial support from the educational institutions and other sources.

Dr. Miller started the Model United Nations at Bethune – Cookman and students from different colleges would participate as ambassadors of foreign countries. I was the ambassador for the United States and this sparked my interest in pursuing a legal career.

Dr. Miller wrote a grant and obtained funding so students were able to travel to the Bahamas for four weeks to study its political system. I, along with several other students which included Guy Molock, now an attorney and minister, accompanied Dr. Miller. As young, rambunctious men our thoughts were more on having fun and meeting girls than studying the Bahamian political institutions. We manage to sneak out on the first night and meet some friends who we knew from college. We had a great time and thought we could get back into the dorm without Dr. Miller knowing what we had done.

It did not work. Dr. Miller was straightforward and frank when he told us if it happened again, we would all be on the plane back to Daytona Beach. With the exception of the drinking water that had a funny after taste, it was an awesome experience. Observing the black Bahamian judges wearing wigs raised my eyebrow. The wigs serve precisely the same purpose as suits, ties, and all other artifice of the court—to present a level of decorum and respect for the process. This isn't a legal issue, but rather a societal one. That said, the wigs are legally required in many nations (no longer in the US, though they used to), but they're essentially just the dress code of the institution, in the same way that no lawyer would be accepted in court without his or her suit.

Dr. Miller died several years ago and I was blessed with the opportunity to speak at his celebration of life. I would often visit him at his adult living facility whenever I traveled to Daytona. He would just light up whenever I walked into his room. The conversation would usually begin with him asking how my family was doing and if I had heard from any other former students. When possible, I would take him out to lunch and he greatly appreciated our fellowship.

Dr. Miller was very compassionate like Dr. Bronson and held a genuine concern for the well- being of others. He sent me $200 to help a family member who was facing criminal charges. Dr. Miller also drove from Daytona Beach to see me graduate from Stetson Law School and he attended my judicial investiture in 2006. I later learned that Dr. and Mrs. Bronson had attempted to come to my investiture as well but had some difficulty with the directions. The administration and professors at Bethune-Cookman remained my college family and I am fortunate to have received their guidance and direction along my journey.

After my first year at B-CC, I returned home to Valdosta during the summer of 1977 to work in the steel mill. I had the house to myself most of the summer as my mother and grandmother had travelled to Lansing, Michigan to visit family there. I managed to save most of my earnings for returning to school in the fall. The summer passed quickly. Dj and I looked forward to returning to campus as upperclassmen and big brothers in the Marching Men of Cookman. I thought a lot about what kind of big brother I would be. Most of my band brothers thought I would really be hard on the freshman because of my experience. Fortunately for them, it was not my nature to be mean spirited to anyone; I rarely harassed them. I had better things to do with my time than harass the freshmen.

I was elected President of the Junior Class, President of the Political-Science Club, and worked hard to make the Dean's List and Presidential Scholar's List. I also pledge Alpha Phi Alpha Fraternity and was President of our pledge line. Combine those activities with band practice and attending class left little time for me to do anything else other than study and sleep. Most evenings, I would be completing term papers in the library until it closed, or typing and studying for exams. In those days, there was no internet or computers to use for writing papers.

DJ and I moved off campus to a duplex at 509 Maple St. It would take us about thirty minutes to walk from our apartment to the campus. As is typical with college students, we loved to have parties on weekends or any night that anyone was willing to appear. We had band brothers who lived under us and we would often have a party going on upstairs and down stairs. Reflecting back, I am amazed at how I was able to have such an active social life and maintain my level of academic excellence.

During my sophomore year, I received my African name, Majadi Mfikiri, from my political science teacher, Dr. Johnson (Chini Koomba). Some of the students in the Political Science Department yearned to connect with our African culture. This led us to take on an African name which was a reflection of our personality. "Majadi Mfikiri" means serious thinker. I loved my name and by my junior senior year, my friends knew me as Majadi and only a few still called me Apache. I gave names to my other friends and fraternity brothers. At the end of my sophomore year, I was pondering where and what would I do after leaving B-CC. I decided in order for me to achieve my full potential while at B-CC, It would be in my best interest to leave the marching band.

I reluctantly decided to have a meeting with Dr. Berry and advise him of my decision. I knew he would not be happy as he expected me to remain committed to the organization. I don't recall what I said to him, but I remember him saying he expected me to be a tuba section leader if I stayed in the band. My mind was made up, and I intended to use my time to prepare for law school and enjoy college life as a non-band member student.

With extra time available, I had no reason to not be involved in every phase of college life. I was also able to obtain several part time and full time jobs while in school. One of those included being a writer and reporter for the Daytona Times, a local black newspaper. I earned $20.00 for each story that was published. My focus was primarily on current events related to the college and community. My articles appeared under my African name," Majadi" and seeing my name in print was like vitamin A to my ego.

DR. JAKE MILLER

1980 SENIOR CLASS
CHAPEL PROGRAM
11:00 A.M.
APRIL 21, 1980

"Words of Wisdom and Truth"
by
SELECTED SENIORS

Guizelous Molock
Division of Humanities
Major: English

James Pierce
Division of Social Sciences
Major: Political Science

Dewanna Williams
"Miss B-CC 1979-80"
Division of Education
Major: Elementary Education

Lynn Thompson
Division of Science &
Mathematics
Major: Biology

Marcia Oban
Division of Business
Major: Marketing

Jackie Cunningham
1980 Senior Class President
Division of Social Sciences
Major: Criminal Justice

CLASS MOTTO

"We've come a long way,
but the challenge is the distance we have to go."

Herbert Rozier and James Pierce at Academic Achievement Day

James Pierce and Wayne Snyder, BCC
Student Government President

James Pierce in New York City with Marching
Men Of Cookman Fall 1976

Marching Men 1977

Chapter Twelve

A setback is a setup for a come back

During my junior year, I decided to run for President of the Student Government Association (SGA). The other two candidates were well known on campus and were from Miami. Wayne Snyder and Gerald Atwell were also members of the marching band, belonged to Greek Letter Organizations, and majored in Political Science. Wayne and I were band freshmen together and we were often classmates in many of the political science courses along with Atwell. Atwell, a saxophone player, entered one year behind us, but was on an accelerated schedule to graduate in three years.

I lost the election to Wayne by 65 votes. Wayne and Gerald were from Miami and a large percentage of the student population hailed from that location. Wayne was also able to garner a lot of support from the football players and I believe that was the difference in the election. I felt very disappointed about losing. However, losing the election was probably the best thing for my legal career. Someone once stated: "A setback is a setup for a comeback." After losing the election, I was determined to go to law school. This meant that I needed to do well on the Law School Admission Test (LSAT).

I spent most of my evenings at the Carl Swisher Library studying for the LSAT and taking practice exams. I also managed to earn some additional income by working in the stock room at Sears. The LSAT day remains indelibly impressed in my mind. I, along with my fraternity brother, Guy Molock, took the exam at Stetson University in Deland. It was during the spring, and the room temperature seemed to border on freezing. The half-day exam left me totally exhausted as I had exerted all of my mental and physical energy to achieve success on the exam. My entire future would depend on how well I had performed the LSAT. After the exam, I was supposed to meet some fraternity brothers and sorority sisters at Stetson and we were planning on going to the Greek Extravaganza at Florida A&M University in Tallahassee.

I was in a daze after the LSAT, and rather than waiting at Stetson to meet the brothers and sisters, I hopped in the car with Guy and headed back to Daytona. At some point, it finally dawned on me that I was supposed to have remained at Stetson and been picked up there for the trip. I had Guy take me back to Deland which was probably about a 20 minute drive. Everyone one was waiting for me, and as I hopped in the van, my finger got caught in the door. Ouch! The LSAT exam left me in a state of confusion along with both physical and emotional distress.

Several months later on a cool spring day, Dr. Miller asked me to stop by his office. I was pleasantly surprised to learn that I had scored the highest grade among Bethune-Cookman students on the LSAT. Shortly thereafter, I learned that I was chosen to participate in the Council on Legal Education Opportunity Pre-law Summer Program along with several of my classmates at the University of Georgia. In addition to the valuable orientation for law school, I would receive a $1,000 scholarship for every semester of Law School. I received this scholarship as a result of an application I completed along with an essay about "Why I Wanted to Attend Law School."

The greatest challenge now was to be accepted into a law school and to figure out how to pay for it. $1,000 would barely be enough to pay for my books for one semester. I did not worry about where the money would come from to pay for my tuition and room and board. I applied to several law schools as the admission process is very competitive and students with the highest LSAT and cumulative grade point average (GPA) were accepted into law school. Law schools would also consider the extra-curricular involvement of the prospective applicant as well.

While my GPA and extra-curricular activities stood out, my LSAT score was not very high despite scoring the highest at my school.

In the spring of 1980, I graduated from Bethune-Cookman College with the highest honors (Magna Cum Laude) in my major, Political Science. We were the first graduating class of the Political Science Department. The graduating seniors included our Student Government President (SGA), Wayne Snyder, Gerald Atwell, who also had unsuccessfully ran for SGA president; Terrye Y. Howell, who would later be elected as a City commissioner of Lake Wales; James A. Zow, who attended and graduated from the University of Florida Law School; and Lori B. James.

It was a beautiful spring day to walk across the podium and receive my degree as my sisters, mother, and Aunt Lona, my father's sister cheered me on. I would be the only child of my mother that received a college degree and among the first few within our entire family. Despite this joyous celebration, my future remained uncertain as I had not received an acceptance from a law school. Several weeks later, I arrived in Athens, Georgia to attend the Council on Legal Education (CLEO) pre-law class.

The classes were quite intimidating and the amount of reading required was overwhelming. The legal terminology was a new language which required constant use of Black's Law Dictionary. Doubts began to creep into my head as to whether my decision to pursue law school was prudent. Analyzing legal cases using the issue, rule, analysis and conclusion (IRAC) approach was not only mentally challenging but physically draining, too.

It was during the pre-law institute that my fellow students and I were introduced to the Socratic Method of Teaching. Developed by the Greek philosopher, Socrates, the Socratic Method is a dialogue between teacher and students, instigated by the continual probing questions of the teacher in a concerted effort to explore the underlying beliefs that shape the students views and opinions. Consequently, we would always be on the edge of our seats while waiting to be called upon by the professor. This required reading the materials and having an understanding of the rules and principles of law to give an intelligent response. I was not alone in feeling academically challenged as my colleagues were experiencing the same doubts and skepticism as we were consumed by the vast depth of the rules of law and its exceptions.

ClEO lasted about four weeks and we all managed to survive the rigorous preparation for law school. Nevertheless, I remained in a state of uncertainty about which law school, if any, would accept me. After leaving Athens, I returned to Valdosta for several days before leaving with my sister, Helen and my brother-in-law to spend the remainder of the summer in Lansing, Michigan. Within several days of job searching, I landed a job with Polk Directory Service. The job required confirming residential addresses and was similar to census taking.

My sister, Helen, allowed me to use her car and I learned my way around Lansing quite well. The highlight of my stay in Lansing was being introduced to Earvin "Magic" Johnson by my cousin, Morris Morrell. Magic had just won his first NBA Title in his rookie season. The NBA title was the final victory for a trifecta which included winning a high school state championship and NCAA Championship. Magic was stretched out in his Mother's living room with his feet resting on a hassock. He was very pleasant and seemed well grounded in light of all his success.

Magic, without any doubt, is my favorite NBA Player of all time. His long career in the NBA and successful entrepreneurial ventures are phenomenal. Moreover, his becoming a spokesperson for Human Immune Deficiency Virus (HIV) raised the level of consciousness through this country and the world in the fight against HIV.

Chapter Thirteen

Paper Chase

The Lord Makes A Way!

Psalms 37:4 KJV states: "Delight thyself also in the Lord; and he shall give thee the desires of thine heart. Growing up in a Christian home provide me with a good foundation for relating to people and circumstances that I would encounter on my journey. Attending Sunday school and church was not a choice in our home but was expected. There have been numerous times during my life when I needed money, or other necessities to make it through. Fortunately, God provided everything I needed, when I needed it. From the time I was born, God had a plan for me to become a lawyer and later a judge. Nothing can stop God's plan for your life.

On August 8th, of 1980, I was admitted to Stetson University College of Law. Finally, the uncertainty and waiting was over. I was excited to tell Dr. Miller and my family about the acceptance letter. The door of opportunity had been opened and now the only remaining concern was paying for tuition, room and board. I did not know where the money would come from but I had faith that the Lord would make a way.

Shortly after receiving my acceptance letter, I received another letter from Stetson's Admission office awarding me a full tuition waiver so long as I maintained good academic status and participated in the minority recruiting program. I also received approval for a Florida

Student Assistant Grant in the amount of $14,000 to pay for my room and board. My dream of becoming an attorney was now within my reach. The rest was up to me. My future looked bright and now it was just a matter of hard work and perseverance. I was overwhelmed with joy when I left Valdosta on a Greyhound Bus to St. Petersburg, Florida. After four years on the Florida east coast, I was on my way to the Florida west coast where the water from the Gulf of Mexico is much clearer, the waves are smaller, and the beaches have finer quartz sand.

Stetson University College of Law is located in Gulfport, Florida. Founded in 1900 as Florida's first law school, Stetson University College of Law has educated outstanding lawyers, judges and other leaders for 115 years. In 1954, the College moved from Stetson's main campus in Deland to Gulfport, nestled in one of the 25 largest metropolitan areas in the United States.

From the school's opening in 1900, the de facto policy of Stetson Law School was not to seek applicants of color but there is no evidence that the school ever denied admission to a black applicant. According to the history recorded in the book, "Florida's First Law School," no blacks applied to Stetson's law school during its first 70 years. In 1971, African-American Thomas Stringer was admitted to the Stetson University College of law and graduated in the spring of 1974, becoming the first black to receive a law degree from Stetson.

In my first year of law classes, there were a total of three African Americans. The other two African Americans were Lewis Whitehead, and Oscar Shaw. Both of these gentlemen were exceptionally brilliant, had previous work experience before entering law school and were older than me. I am certain that each of them were in the top ten percent of our class.

It was not until many years after law school that I discovered Oscar's dad, Justice Leander Shaw, was a member of the Florida Supreme Court. Oscar seemed to have so much knowledge about the cases and was very well spoken in class. I admire him for being so humble about his background and never mentioning it to me or anyone else to my knowledge.

There were only two other African Americans in the entire student body at Stetson. They were both in their third year and graduating in the spring. There was very little interaction between African American students and we each seemed to prefer it that way.

Law students are responsible for completing massive amounts of reading on a daily basis, and law professors employ unique methods of teaching -- such as the Socratic Method -- that are unfamiliar to students in any other discipline. These features acknowledge that success in law school cannot be achieved based on intelligence alone, but also through implementation. My first year of law school was the most rigorous and challenging academic experience in my life with the exception of the Florida Bar Examination.

Law school can be extremely discouraging because students receive very little feedback during the school year. Classes are graded solely upon final exam scores. Mid-term exams, graded papers, and credit for class participation were non-existent. I was unsure whether I was grasping the concepts sufficiently and was able to demonstrate knowledge of those concepts to the professors.

I had doubts concerning my ability to compete with the brightest graduates from Ivey League schools, and other major colleges and universities throughout the United States since I had attended a small historically black college. I was determined that although I may not be the brightest student in my class, I would be the hardest worker and no one would study more than me.

My typical day would consist of waking up at 6:00 a.m., having breakfast in the cafeteria and studying several hours before class. My dinner would normally consist of gorging myself at a buffet style restaurant located within walking distance in the Pasadena shopping center as I did not have a vehicle.

I would then spend the remainder of my day either in class or in the library until it closed around 11:00 p.m. I would then return to my room on campus and study until I could no longer keep my eyes open. My roommate, Daniel Consuegra, was much older than me and seemed to have a good grasp on the legal topics. Dan graduated from the University of Maryland and today he is the managing partner of his law firm that consists of more than 40 lawyers and 400 support staff which represents creditors.

Dan and I got along well. The only issue I had with him was explaining to him why I did not like to be called "Jimbo." Otherwise, sharing a dorm room together was pleasant. For the first time, people referred to me as Jim. Over the last several years in college, I became known to most of my college mates as Majadi. The other significant difference between law school and college was the student demographics. I went from attending a predominantly black college to a law school that only had five African Americans including me. Fortunately, my Jr. High and high school integration experiences assisted me in making this cultural change easy.

I also managed to make some lifelong friends in the Stetson Intramural Basketball league and in the library. The league provided a nice break from my life as a book worm and our team, "Fastbreak" won the league championship all six semesters that we were there. The members of our team were Mike Pieri, Jim Zack, John Phillips, Jeff Sherman, Jim Heptner, Bob Wahl, and our ringer, a semi-professional player that played in Europe, Paul Molleni. Paul was the only member of the team that was not in law school. However, his wife Susan was a classmate of ours.

I met one of my brightest and best lifelong friends in the Stetson Law Library. Danell and Tom Deberg decided to go to law school together while raising their three minor children, Benjamin, Dana, and Allison. Danell was from New Jersey and graduated from the Worcester City Hospital School of Nursing. She received her nursing degree from the University of Wisconsin at Madison. She moved to Florida to attend law school at Stetson after her parents retired to Ft. Myers.

Danell was definitely one of the most brilliant and most down to earth persons I had ever met. She had this huge smile and whenever she laughed, you knew without a doubt, it was her. Without any hesitation,

Danell and Tom welcomed me into their homes and at their dinner table for Thanksgiving and Christmas meals. They were just "good people."

We have remained friends for over 34 years and I consider all of them to be family. One of her colleagues stated "It is rare to see a person who leads such a compassionate life, all by example. Danell does not seek accolades and was visibly embarrassed discussing all that she does for others. To say that she is extremely humble would be an under-statement."

Danell has traveled all over the world with a group of non-denominational Christian medical missionaries. They deliver primary healthcare in areas which are under served, have no healthcare or have been struck by natural disasters. Danell has witnessed horrific conditions and a "magnitude of suffering." While in India, she encountered people living on the streets, many of whom had gangrene, tuberculosis, and leprosy. The members of her group are often the first white people that have visited that community.

Danell is the brightest and most selfless person I have ever met. She was ranked number two in our graduating law class. Her compassion also extends to the local community where she worked in the St. Pete Free Clinic for eight years until it closed. She continues to work at the Beacon House, the homeless shelter associated with the Free Clinic and has a home in Belize where she is faithfully involved in mission work for the local community.

She can often be found at St. Vincent's Soup Kitchen with children from her church, Garden of Peace Lutheran, after cooking food to help feed the homeless. The respect for her is summed up best by her son and law partner, Ben Deberg: "If you don't know what the right thing to do is, you just wait and see what Danell does." I would not have submitted an application for appointment to a vacant judicial seat which occurred when Judge Karl Krube retired, but for Danell urging me to apply. Danell is not only my first child's godmother, but she was like a big sister to me. I give her much credit for inspiring me to pursue an appointment to the judiciary of the 6th Judicial Circuit.

Danell clerked for a federal judge before entering private practice. Danell would later be the lead trial attorney in a malpractice lawsuit on behalf of my younger brother's sister-in-law who almost died after being admitted into the hospital for a routine tubal ligation. As a result of an infection, the patient went into a coma and her right arm was amputated. Danell prepared the case for trial and negotiated a settlement against the hospital and doctors. The client received lump sum payments and a life time annuity. She was recognized by the St. Petersburg Bar Association as a "Hero Among Us" and still volunteers to help where ever there is a need.

My first semester at Stetson went quickly and I had little if any contact with anyone outside of the campus. I managed to travel to Tampa for the annual Florida Classic Football game between Bethune-Cookman College and Florida A&M University and experienced a great 16-14 Wildcat victory over the Rattlers. Then it was back to school to continue studying for the first semester final exams.

Several days before the final exams, I fell ill to a serious toothache. I had occasionally experienced the pain before and normally it would gradually subside. I had put off taking care of my teeth because I did not have dental insurance and knew it would be expensive. The pain was very agonizing and I could no longer concentrate on my studies. It completely dulled my thinking and I knew there was no way I could perform well on the exams without receiving dental care and alleviating the deep throbbing pain.

I managed to locate a dentist in St. Petersburg and received a root canal. The most painful part was receiving the pain medication through a needle. I had an infection and it was necessary to treat that before having the procedure. After the drilling and packing, my head felt as if it was going to explode. Nevertheless, it was better than the unrelenting toothache pain which rendered me helpless. I just wanted to feel better in time for the exams.

I utilized every resource in preparation for the final exams—student outlines, my outlines and notes and any other material that would help. I felt confident going into the exams that I had put in the time and read all the required cases. Now it was all about demonstrating my knowledge of the rules of law, exceptions, analysis and conclusions. I made sure I got a good night rest before the exams and had a nutritious meal. The exams for each course were all essay questions and lasted several hours or more. I felt I did well enough to pass all of the courses but much depended upon the grading curve. We would not receive the exam results until several weeks later when they would be posted on a student information Board in the breeze way.

My main objective was to avoid being placed on academic probation and keep my tuition waiver. This seemed to be a reasonably attainable goal coming from a small historically black college and competing against the best and brightest from the other major colleges and universities. I believed that studying longer and better preparation for the final exams would make up for my intellectual or academic deficiencies. I was determined not to let anyone work harder than me.

I was particularly concerned about Contracts, where Professor Kuenzel was known for giving a D grade to one fourth of the class. When I saw my grade of C in his class, I felt as though I had made a B. Likewise, my C+ in Torts from Professor O'leck was a pleasant surprise. I survived my first semester of law school without a D and avoided academic probation. I felt as though I had made the honor roll and now had confidence that I could compete and survive in my new academic environment.

My second semester was even better as I earned a B in Torts. Torts involved litigation for personal wrongs and injuries. I decided to attend summer school after successfully completing my first year of law school. Summer school was less intense and I only took two courses. After earning a B in Corporations and a C in constitutional Law, I felt good about law school and my ability to finish successfully.

Chapter Fourteen

LEGAL ASSISTANT

After surviving my first year of law school, I thought it was important to gain some legal experience and work for a law firm. Students were allowed to work in their second year and I could certainly use the extra money. My first legal assistant job was for Jacobs, Robbins & Gaynor, a law firm in St. Petersburg.

I do not recall how I learned about them or how I got the job. I probably was there less than a week or two before I met Herman (Buzzy) Blumenthal, while shooting hoops on the basketball court. I had seen Buzzy on several other occasions while I worked at the Family Mart Liquor store which was several blocks from of the law school campus.

Buzzy was a Stetson Law School graduate and was building a practice in the areas of personal injury law, family law, and probate. He lived just a few blocks from the law school in a beautiful Spanish designed home in Gulfport and his law office was located in nearby Seminole. We instantly became friends and he asked me if I stilled worked at the liquor store. I told him that I had recently started working for Jacobs, Robbins, & Gaynor in St. Petersburg. He offered me a legal assistant position with his firm and without hesitation, I accepted. After explaining to him that I did not have a car, he indicated that was not a problem.

Buzzy was an excellent business man and had a thriving personal injury practice. I learned much from him about professionalism and the practice of law. He loved basketball and on July 4th, 1982 we were playing pickup basketball at Sunset Park in Pasadena. Two prominent local African American attorneys, Daryl Rouson and Darryl Flannigan were also hooping and enjoying an early morning run of outdoor basketball in the park.

It was a typical hot, muggy 4th of July and we were going up and down the court when Buzzy suddenly went down on the concrete. He was unable to stand or put any weight on his right leg and we had to carry him to his vehicle. After being examined at the hospital, he was diagnosed with a torn Achilles tendon. His injury would require surgery to repair the tear and a full length cast from his hip to his foot. As a result of his injury, I had to become his driver for all of his appointments and in essence his chauffeur. He was always very generous and never failed to buy me lunch whenever we were together. I became part of their family and sat at their dinner table on many occasions. Buzzy's wife, Linda, would later give Valencia, my wife, a baby shower when we were expecting our first child.

Buzzy paid me well and did not hesitate whenever I needed a loan or additional money for expenses. He helped me obtain a bank loan to purchase a 1974 Ghia Mustang which I drove until I began working for the Public Defender's office. I was not only his law clerk but personal assistant. We remain friends to this day.

Often times, after an evening of studying, Danell and I would go over to their house when they were out of town and raid their refrigerator. They were happy that we did. They are really two beautiful spirits and certainly two of my most loving and generous friends. After I left my employment with Buzzy to take a job with the Public Defender's office, he generously gave me his 1974 Pontiac Grandville convertible which was very well kept and still running good. It was a beautiful Cherry red color with mag rims and a white rag top. My colleagues in the public defender office loved that car as we would all pile into it and go to lunch with the top down. It could easily seat seven people comfortably. Buzzy and Linda are warm hearted good people that made a difference for me along my journey.

ATTORNEY MICHAEL SIEGEL AND COLONEL IVAN SHERARD

JAMES PIERCE AND HERMAN BLUMENTHAL III

Chapter Fifteen

Nuptials

While at Stetson, I also became friends with Bob and Sylvia Morse. Bob's light complexion, curly black hair, bushy eyebrows, moustache and genteel personality were all the ingredients of a lady's man. Bob was a minister and law student at Stetson after graduating from Harvard University. Bob provided me with my first social connections to the St. Petersburg community. He served as the interim minister at First Baptist Institutional Church and introduced me to my wife, Valencia Wilson.

Valencia, a Godly woman, was born in St. Petersburg, graduated from Lakewood High School and attended Tuskegee Institute. We dated for several years while I attended law school. She was employed as a paraprofessional in the Pinellas County School System. During my last semester of law school, I proposed to Valencia in Campbell Park.

I completed my course work at Stetson and received my Juris Doctorate Degree on May 14th, 1983. It was a beautiful spring day and many family members were in town to witness this momentous occasion and our marriage. Dr. Miller had driven over from Daytona Beach and was beaming with pride to see one of his students receiving a law degree from Stetson University College of Law.

Valencia and I had a lot faith but little means. I managed to get a bank loan with Buzzy as a co-signer that allowed me to purchase our wedding rings and rent an apartment. We exchanged wedding vows, on May 15, 1983, the day after I graduated from Stetson Law School. Since my relatives were in town for the graduation, we decided to get married while they were here. Receiving my Juris Doctorate Degree and our marriage the following day was a phenomenal experience. We had much to celebrate with family and friends.

We exchanged our vows at Valencia's mother's home and had a wedding reception at the St. Petersburg International Folk Fair Society building following the ceremony. My brother, Alfred, was my best man. Following the reception, we drove to Sarasota Beach for our honeymoon. From our union, we were blessed with two wonderful children, Veronica, born January 3, 1985; and James Benjamin, born November 15, 1988.

Sylvia met Bob while he was in law school and immediately their passion was ignited. Sylvia hailed from a prominent St. Petersburg family and her brother published the *Weekly Challenger*, a publication targeted for the black community. Bob was a brilliant orator, delivering his sermons with passion and fervor for the Lord. He was positively charged and loved to make everyone laugh. He was an awesome brother who would bless you with whatever he had. Bob and Sylvia were the proto-type couple of the 80s. Sylvia worked in the real estate department for the City of St. Petersburg. They lived in a beautiful condominium on the Inter-coastal Waterway in Pasadena. Many wonderful times were spent with them enjoying dinner in their home in the sky.

Unfortunately, Bob succumbed to leukemia during the spring of 1983, after a long and valiant fight to survive. Sylvia would later graduate from Stetson Law School and establish a real estate law practice in Sarasota. I am thankful for the privilege of knowing them as they made a difference for me while I was a law student.

Chapter Sixteen

THE BAR

During my last semester at Stetson, I only needed several credits for graduation and I decided that I would use my extra time to study for the Florida Bar Examination. You were required to pass the Florida Bar Examination before you could be licensed as an attorney to practice law. This included passing a background check as well as an ethics exam and two days of testing on substantive and procedural law. One day was dedicated to Florida law and given in an essay format. The Multi-state examination was a multiple choice format. I heard many stories about students who had graduated from law school but could not pass the state bar examination. I did not want to be one of them and I could not afford to take the exam again because it was expensive. Consequently, I put all my energy into passing the exam the first time. I wore out a stool from sitting and studying in it. I would often take practice exams to become familiar with the anticipated subject areas.

It was necessary to travel to Orlando to take the exam and fortunately for me, I had relatives that were willing to let me stay with them over night. Ellis and Louise Grant had owned a furniture store in Orlando for many years and welcome me into their home. My grandmother was Cousin Ellis' Aunt and they would often visit us in Valdosta. They were very accommodating and took good care of me.

On the night before the first day of examination, my head was so full of legal mumbo jumbo that I could not fall asleep. I knew how important it was to show up for the exam well rested but my mind was so clogged with principles of law and exceptions that I could not rest. I figured I would just lay there with closed eyes. I was frustrated and could not believe that I would not be able to demonstrate how much I knew because of my lack of sleep. Fortunately, my adrenaline was so high when I started the exam, that the lack of sleep did not affect my mental faculties. The exam was challenging but I was confident and prepared. It wore me out but I slept much better the second night.

After completing the second day of the exams, a huge amount of weight was lifted off my shoulders. The ethics exam was only several hours. It was multiple- choice and not very difficult if you remembered the rules on not commingling your money with your client, avoiding conflict of interests and maintaining client confidentiality. After completing the examinations, it would take several months or more to receive the results.

On September 12, 1983, the Multistate Bar Examination scores were released and a scaled score of 131 or higher passed. I was thrilled to see my passing score of 136 and proud to share this news with family and friends. My passing ethics score would follow shortly in which I correctly answered 45 of the 50 questions. Upon receiving my test scores, I immediately called The Honorable Judge James Sanderlin, the first African American Judge in the 6th Judicial Circuit and asked him to swear me in as an attorney for the State of Florida. He graciously obliged and I took the Attorney oath in the St. Petersburg Court House as Valencia held our family Bible. Attorney James Vincent Pierce had arrived in the legal profession.

The door of opportunity had been opened by God and I was gracious for where I had come from and where I stood when I was admitted to the Bar. The many years of study and hard work had paid off. I was excited about practicing law and becoming a trial attorney. I immediately applied for a job with the Hillsborough State Attorney Office without success. My second interview was with the Public Defender of Pinellas/Pasco County.

Mr. Robert E. Jagger was the longest serving Public Defender in the nation. Many prominent attorneys and judges are by products of the Public Defender and State Attorney office. Mr. Jagger was a lot of fun and allowed you to manage and litigate your cases as you deemed appropriate. Always in a jolly spirit and ready to talk about any case, he loved lawyering. He also loved to tell us stories about how his office started and the many people that had worked in his office. Many of whom had matriculated to the bench like the Honorable Susan Schaffer who would serve as Chief Judge, and many other prominent trial lawyers.

Judge Frank White was one of those persons. Valencia and I had our reception at Judge White and Mrs. White's home. Mr. Jagger held great favor for Judge White, and I may have been the beneficiary of that fondness. I believe that I have given my best on every job in my life and proven my value in the work place. However, it does not hurt to know someone who knows someone. The value of networking would play a key role in receiving an appointment to the judiciary.

Chapter Seventeen

Public Defense

There was a vibrant spirit of camaraderie in Public Defender's Office of the Sixth Judicial Circuit. Whenever an attorney would win a trial, you earned the right to have the bone and skull flag hang outside your office until another attorney won a trial. So the flag would be continually passed to the most recent victorious trial attorney. There existed a harmonious spirit of cooperation among the attorneys and we often would discuss our theories of the case and evidence with each other. After several years of trying misdemeanor and juvenile cases, I was promoted to the felony division.

My career in the Public Defender's office blossomed after successfully defending and winning numerous misdemeanor jury trials. Shortly after being promoted to the felony division, I was assigned to my first murder trial. My responsibility was to prepare a motion to suppress the defendant's statements.

It was necessary for me to fly to Los Angeles, California to take the sworn statements of several law enforcement officers who were involved with the arrest of the co-defendants. The transition as a Public Defender went smoothly until I parked my 1974 Grandville Pontiac in Judge Grube's parking space.

I pulled into the parking space in an apparent oblivious state and did not realize that I had parked in the Judge's parking space. After realizing what I had done, I experienced agony and grief. Judge Grube used his vehicle to block me in and I knew this could only mean trouble for the knuckle head who parked in the Judge' s spot. That would be me, your honor. All of these thoughts were going through my head about being reprimanded or held in contempt of court.

After presenting my body before Judge Grube with a quick apology, he was ever so kind. He said, "Oh! It's no problem. I'll go down and move my vehicle so you can get out." Not only was Judge Grube very nice to me but 20 years later I would be appointed to his judicial seat, Group 10. I think God was trying to tell me something when I parked in Judge Grube's spot and this was His plan for me. The odds of how this occurred are infinitum and the only explanation for me is divine intervention. I later learned that Judge Grube had shared office space with Buzzy and some of the other lawyers in the same building. Perhaps he recognized Buzzy's vehicle and that is why he was not angry with me for taking his parking space.

I enjoyed my several days in Los Angeles and San Diego, California. Despite losing the motion to suppress the defendant's statements, Mr. Jagger complimented me on my courtroom performance. The defendant was acquitted by the appellate court due to a jury instruction error committed by the presiding judge. The defendant could not be tried again because of the 5th Amendment protection from double jeopardy. Double jeopardy is a procedural defense that forbids a defendant from being tried again on the same or similar charges in the same case following a legitimate acquittal or conviction by the same governmental agency.

Our client was allegedly the mastermind in a plot to kill and steal from her employer and her daughter and boyfriend carried out the plan. The victim's finger was severed and her diamond ring was taken. The co-defendants were arrested in San Diego. I had never been to the West Coast. I took the walk down Hollywood Boulevard gazing at the names of celebrities and managed to drive by the Lakers Forum. I managed to survive negotiating six lanes of travel on the interstate and arrive timely at my depositions.

Other than the Assistant State Attorney, Larry Sandefer, objecting to me recording the depositions of the witnesses, the sworn statements proceeded as expected. I appreciated my role as a defense attorney and gave my best effort to represent my client. After successfully defending numerous felony and misdemeanor cases, I was promoted to the position of Division Director and assigned to the Capital Litigation Team. Capital cases involved the possibility of the death penalty or life in prison. Along with the promotions came significant increases in my salary.

My years as an Assistant Public Defender provided many opportunities to develop and hone my skills as a trial attorney. My favorite part of a jury trial was jury selection. Jury selection is an interesting process and involves a process of elimination as opposed to selection. The lawyers and parties decide who to eliminate and the jury is composed of whoever is left on the panel. I developed the skill of memorizing the names of the entire panel before I addressed each one individually in voire dire. The prospective panel could have as many 50 or more jurors for consideration. "Voire dire" is a Latin term which means to "see and to say."

One of the most important lessons I learned is that you try cases with the expectation of winning but also to make a record for appellate review. Fortunately for several of my clients, the appellate record which I made on the trial level resulted in the reversal of their life sentences. One of my client's cases was reversed several times by the Appellate Court based on improper arguments by the Assistant State Attorney. The defendant entered a plea of no contest as we were about to retry the case for a third time and he received a more favorable sentence.

As a defense attorney, you had to be on the cutting edge of the law and use every resource available to defend your client and their rights under the state and federal constitutions. The trial was your client's only day in court and my job was to insure that my client received a fair trial and the State proved the case beyond every reasonable doubt.

As an Assistant Public Defender for 6th Judicial Circuit, I was Lead trial counsel on more than 100 criminal jury trials from January of 1984 through April of 1995. I was Board Certified as criminal trial attorney in 1995. I Served as Division Director of Several court divisions and supervised eight attorneys and staff. As a member of the capital litigation team, I represented more than 50 individuals charge with First Degree Murder and successfully defended 12 defendants in death penalty sentencing phases. After being assigned to career criminal division, I represented hundreds of defendants charged as habitual felony offenders.

While assigned to the habitual felony division within the Office of the Public Defender, I drafted and argued a motion challenging the constitutionality of Florida's Habitual Felony Offender Statute. The motion was based on the grounds that it violated the 14th Amendment due process and equal protection clause as applied to defendants assigned to the career criminal division. A disparate amount of African Americans were being assigned to the career criminal division and the motion was made to dismantle the division as it had a discriminatory impact. Although the motion was denied, it raised the level of consciousness regarding how cases are assigned to the career criminal division. I represented several other defendants who were charged with capital crimes in challenging cases.

One of those clients, Joseph Glover, a diagnosed paranoid schizophrenic, was charged with two counts of First Degree Murder. The defendant had been previously found incompetent due to mental illness and committed to a state mental hospital prior to the murders. After release from the state mental hospital, Mr. Glover's behavior grew increasingly bizarre.

The children, Michelle Morris, 14, and her brother, Eddie, 12, were stabbed to death during the early morning hours of April 21, 1986 and found in the bath tub by their mother. Their bodies were nearly decapitated. Glover was connected to the crime scene through bite marks found on the victims, a bloody foot print and other evidence. He was arrested nine days after the murders and prosecutors sought the death penalty in the case. This case was significant because of community outrage for the vicious murder of two children in their St. Petersburg home and it certainly did not help that Glover was African American. Add his confession to that scenario and this case is what we referred to in the Public Defender's office as a "burner." This meant that the case had the potential for a death sentence.

A year after the murders, a circuit judge found Glover incompetent to stand trial, and he was sent to a state mental institution. A year later, several psychiatrists decided Glover was mentally fit to stand trial. The case was assigned to me. The murder of two children is a very challenging case for any experienced lawyer, and even more challenging for a less experienced lawyer like me. The potential for the death penalty made the case even more complicated.

The most valuable resource a defense attorney has in a capital case is time. My anticipated defense would be not guilty by reason of insanity as Glover was responding to the voices of spirits which caused him to do things beyond his control. I knew this would be a tough defense for a jury to accept and that an experienced seasoned prosecutor such as Douglas Crow could easily persuade a jury that Glover knew the difference between right and wrong when he nearly decapitated two defenseless children. Regardless of the fact that at age 20, Glover had complained to police that "evil spirits" were making him do things.

I took a pro-active posture in the case, and bombarded the state with numerous lengthy motions attacking the constitutionality of the death penalty and began preparing an insanity defense. If Joseph Glover was going to be executed, the State would have to prove he was sane at the time of the murders and that the aggravating factors in the case outweighed the mitigating factors. Fortunately, the court realized that accepting a no contest plea with imposition of two consecutive life sentences without the possibility of parole for 50 years would save the state substantial expenses for trial and appeals. Most people do not realize that it costs millions of dollars in legal fees in order to execute a convicted murderer. Mr. Glover was fortunate to have Judge Claire Luten presiding over his case.

I tried many cases in front of Judge Luten and while she did not hesitate to hand out a tongue lashing or an off cuff remark, I believe she was one of the fairest judges I ever encountered. She encouraged me to become active with the State Bar Association Criminal Rules Procedure and I rose in the ranks from a committee chairperson to becoming the Vice Chairperson for the Florida Rules of Criminal Procedure for the State of Florida. That happened after the Glover trial had been long resolved. I was disappointed that Judge Luten lost her election because she was a very knowledgeable trial judge and efficiently managed her caseloads.

After the Glover case, I would represent 12 other defendants that were convicted of First Degree Murder in which the State would seek the death penalty. I would end my career with a perfect 12 and 0 record, winning every case without a death penalty recommendation by the jury. This resulted in spite of a defendant who asked the jury to give him the death penalty during the penalty phase sentencing trial. The defendant dismissed my co-counsel, Kandice Friesen and I from his case after he was convicted of first degree murder.

Buddy Granger who was charged with killing his ex-wife's boyfriend by shooting him in the chest and between the eyes, surprised the victim while he was on the phone with Judith Granger. "Get out! Get out!" the ex-wife heard victim say. Then the phone went dead. Prosecutors said the murder ended the dangerous obsession of an ex-husband. The Grangers had been married twice. Granger had followed his ex-wife's vehicle to the victim's house. The victim had exchanged cars with her and this may have saved her life.

After Granger was convicted of First Degree Murder, he insisted on representing himself. Judge Schaffer tried to talk him out of it, saying she thought he would regret it. When Granger insisted, Judge Schaffer gave her approval, noting she had no choice under Florida law. During the penalty phase, Granger argued to the jury the day's purpose was to decide "what to do with Buddy Granger." "It boils down to dying in prison or dying in the electric chair," he said.

"I'm telling you that Buddy Granger would prefer the quicker death in the Florida electric chair, and I hope that's the verdict you will bring back," he said.

Prosecutors asked for the death penalty, noting Granger's armed robbery conviction and that he killed the victim while committing a burglary. Assistant State attorney Bob Heyman said Granger – who for many years had gambling problems and once underwent treatment at a hospital – still doesn't know where to put his chips. Jurors heard "the desperate ramblings of a convicted robber and a convicted murderer," Heyman told the press afterwards.

After the jury returned a recommendation for life, Judge Schaffer told Granger that she suspected he didn't really want the death penalty – that he was "rolling the dice" for a new trial. She said she believed he knew a death sentence would automatically be sent to the Florida Supreme Court for review.

The closest call I had for one of my clients receiving the death penalty was a 6 to 6 vote in the case of Sharon Bailey. Bailey, a 32 year old African American woman, was charged with beating a 70 year old retired schoolteacher to death with a glass figurine that weighed 12 to 15 pounds. Bailey pummeled the victim, leaving her with 124 wounds, including broken ribs, a broken nose, a split lip, and two bite marks on her arm. Every rib in the victim's body was broken and she died because there was nothing to support her chest or lungs.

Bailey took the victim's car, jewelry, credit cards and her checkbook. She pawned the victim's $8,900 engagement ring for $200 – after breaking the victim's finger to get it off her hand. My Co-counsel Barry Cobb and I knew this case could be a "burner." We decided that if the case was tried, it was likely that our defense of voluntary intoxication would not be accepted by the jury. We decided to split the case and have one lawyer do the guilt portion of the trial and the second lawyer would handle the penalty phase. Our reasoning was that the jury would be more likely to recommend life if the guilt phase lawyer was not the same for the penalty phase.

We further agreed to have the guilt phase lawyer ask questions pertaining to the guilt phase and the penalty phase lawyer ask questions pertaining to the penalty phase. This resulted in a two day jury selection process and did not go over well with Judge Schaffer to put it mildly. Judge Susan Schaffer was a brilliant attorney and Judge who graduated number one in her law class at Stetson University. She was a living legend in her own time and went on to hold the position of chief judge for many years in the 6th Judicial Circuit.

Needless to say, she was not enamored with Barry and I for using so much time in jury selection. She called us to the bench as we were ending the second day of jury selection and said, "I see I'm going to have a problem with you two. After this trial you let Mr. Jagger know that there will be only one lawyer conducting jury selection, not two." And with her admonition, we proceeded to try our case as we had planned. Our strategy worked to perfection. One more vote for the death penalty and Sharon Bailey would have been on death row in the Florida State Prison system. As a side point, she filed an ineffective assistance claim against Barry and me afterwards because we lost the guilt portion of the trial. I am not sure if she realized that we saved her life but appeals in any criminal case are par for the course. You can expect defendants to blame their lawyers whenever they are found guilty. Seldom does anyone go quietly without protest to prison.

There are many other cases I could discuss which I tried with my colleagues David Parry, a prominent defense attorney in the Tampa Bay Area and other Assistant Public Defenders such as the legendary Ronald Eide. I am thankful that I had the opportunity to watch Ron Eide try cases and have him as a mentor. Ron was amazing at winning cases which were not winnable. His silver tongue, blond hair and dynamic physique apparently caused the jurors to focus on what he said and not so much on the evidence presented by the prosecution. Ron retired about a year ago after a stellar career in the Public Defender's Office.

Chapter Eighteen

Bench Debacle

After trying more than 100 criminal jury trials, representing numerous habitual felony offenders, and representing numerous defendants charged with First Degree Murder, I decided to apply for appointment to the bench of the 6th Judicial Circuit. I was confident that with my more than ten years of experience trying serious felony cases and being a managing attorney, that this was an attainable goal.

There are two ways you can become a judge in the state of Florida, by appointment by the governor to an interim vacancy or by election. I chose the appointment process because it was less expensive and you had to convince less people that you were qualified to be a judge. Eventually if you are appointed, you would have to stand for election every six years after you complete your appointed term.

If you run for election, you are required to pay the filing fee which was approximately $6,000 for Circuit Court and then you have to convince a majority of the voters in the Circuit which includes Pasco County and Pinellas to elect you. The nominating process does not cost anything but requires you to submit an application to the Judicial Nominating Commission (JNC)for the 6th Judicial Circuit. The JNC is comprised of members from the community, governor appointments and Florida Bar appointments.

The appointment process is essentially convincing the members of the JNC to select you for an interview and after reviewing your application, nominate you to Governor for appointment along with as many as nine other applicants. The Governor will then interview the short list of applicants and make the appointment.

In order to receive an interview, candidates seek recommendation letters from members in the legal community and community in general which supports the candidate's application and qualifications to serve as a judge. I was able to receive an interview with the JNC on all five of my applications. I really did not expect to come out of the committee on my first application and I viewed it as a networking and learning experience. I felt better about the second application but once again I was not recommended by the JNC as a nominee for appointment by the Governor.

Finally, on the third application for appointment to a County Court position, I was nominated by the Judicial Nominating Commission (JNC) for appointment by Florida Governor Lawton Chiles. The other two nominees were Assistant County Attorney Myra Scott McNary and my co-worker, Senior Assistant Public Defender, Nora McClure. I was elated to receive the nomination with my colleagues.

In the 1990s, women began to experience an increase in their appointment as judges along with a renewed interest in uncovering underlying discrimination. The National Organization for Women and the National Association of Women Judges banded together to push the state and federal courts to review a perceived bias against women that they believed existed in the courts.

Nora and Myra were very qualified and either one would be an easy choice for the governor. There were no African American judges on the bench in the 6th Judicial Circuit after the retirement of Judge James Sanderlin and Judge Frank White.

Appointments are supposed be non-partisan as are judicial elections in Florida. Aspiring candidates running for election and judges are prohibited from attending party functions and it is a misdemeanor to disclose party affiliations.

I knew my fellow nominees very well and held each of them in high regard. The McNary's were members at the Mt. Carmel Baptist Church where my family and I also attended. Myra's husband, Lavaughn and I were good friends, and teammates in a three on three basketball church tournament which we won.

Lavaughn and I were also charter members Omicron Beta Lambda graduate chapter of the Alpha Phi Alpha Fraternity. On one occasion, I helped the McNary's family move from their apartment to their new home.

Nora and I worked in the same office and our relationship had always been amiable and it has remained that way throughout our careers. I have nothing but great things to say about either of them and believe we all had the qualities to become a good judge.

I decided to travel to Tallahassee and do whatever I could to convince Governor Chiles to appoint me. I was able to make it into the Governor's office for a bill signing with the help of Representative Peter Rudy Wallace, speaker of the House and a Pinellas County official.

I was confident that my introduction to the Governor would certainly not hurt and he might remember me when he made the appointment. I did not know that he had appointed Myra McNary to fill former Judge Mary Mcallister's vacancy on the previous day. Governor Chiles' appointment of Judge McNary made her the first African American woman judge in the 6th Judicial Circuit.

While I was happy for Judge McNary and her family, I experienced melancholy after not receiving the appointment. It seemed as though I was so close but in retrospect, it was not my time. I often tell the story how I became a part of history by losing to the first African American woman to sit as a judge in the 6th Judicial Circuit. Judge McNary was challenged several times during her bid for re-election. I am not sure if I would have been as successful in an election as Judge McNary. Despite my disappointment, I decided to keep pursuing an appointment.

Another judicial vacancy occurred shortly afterward Judge McNary's appointment. After making the short list for the Governor's consideration of appointment but not receiving the appointment, I remained optimistic. The fourth interview was unlike the others. During the interview, I was confronted with a letter from an anonymous person which questioned my fitness to serve as a judge.

The last thing a judicial candidate needs is derogatory comments to the JNC. The letter was written out of spite and malice to derail my appointment and it worked. The suggestion was made that I believed my race would assist me in receiving the nomination because there was a dire need for African American judges. Additionally, the poison pen letter suggested I was a womanizer and gambler.

Being questioned about the contents of a letter from an anonymous person is frustrating because you are unable to address the content of the letter since the author hides behind anonymity. I was blindsided by a coward and totally humiliated when asked by the JNC to explain the allegations. It was not fair that I was confronted with allegations from an anonymous person without any notice. Most people agree that the best reaction to a positive pen letter is no reaction.

The positive thing out of that incident was the creation of the Pierce Rule which does not allow the JNC to consider an anonymous letter. My quest for the bench was undermined by anonymous letter fraught with innuendo and assaults on my character. The effects of the letter on the Judicial Nomination Commission members were devastating. I was not recommended by the JNC for consideration by the Governor. My quest for the bench was thwarted and hindered, and there was nothing I could do.

After the fourth application, I decided to not apply again. I was humiliated with the process and decided to put my quest for the bench on the back burner. I also decided to pursue a career change to gain some valuable civil practice experience.

There was also much uncertainty in the Public Defender's office as Mr. Jagger was being challenged by a prominent defense attorney and former Assistant Public Defender, Robert Dillinger. While no one pressured employees to become active in Mr. Jagger's campaign, to me and some others in the office, it seemed like the right thing to do if you held a position of leadership.

Active involvement in the election could be good or really bad depending on the outcome. If you were on the side of the winning candidate, life and employment would continue as usual. However, if not, you could be without employment. Mr. Jagger lost the election to Bob Dilinger and several individuals lost their jobs after heckling during one of Mr. Dilinger's campaign activities. There were other supporters of Mr. Jagger that were not terminated by Mr. Dilinger after he won the election. I had left the Public Defender's office when the election occurred and did not have to endure the stress of those who had remained in the Public Defender's Office.

JAMES PIERCE AND MICHAEL TARVER

Chapter Nineteen

Civil Law

I was made aware that State Farm was creating an in house law firm to represent State Farm Insurance Company and State Farm insureds. Although I had limited civil experience, I had substantial trial experience. My interview with Kevin Korth went well and he offered me a job subject to passing a drug screening. The only problem was that I would have to take a $5,000 pay cut in salary. However, Kevin assured me that this would only be temporary and if I performed well, salary increases and bonuses would occur frequently. Mr. Jagger was known for saying "Change is good, even if it's bad."

If you do not choose to take a chance in life, you will never experience a change. It was refreshing to practice a new area of law. Assistant Public Defenders often received a bad rap from their clients and are often perceived as being less capable or talented as private lawyers or as defendants call them "street lawyers." The truth of the matter is that there is good and bad in almost everything and some of the best criminal defense lawyers I have ever known either worked in the Public Defender's Office or are former Assistant Public Defenders that are now members of the judiciary.

Suddenly with my career change, I went from representing the indigent accused to representing a billion dollar corporation and its insureds. The availability of expert witnesses and resources was seemingly unlimited. State Farm was not hesitant to spend thousands of dollars defending a case if it required them to do so rather than pay a claim which in their estimation was not owed.

The State Farm motto was "We pay what we owe, nothing more, nothing less." As an associate of Kevin Korth & Associates, employees of State Farm Mutual Insurance Company, it was not long before I was in court trying automobile negligence cases. Defending an insurance company or an insured is akin to being a prosecutor in a criminal case. If you look hard and long enough at a plaintiff's case you can always find weaknesses in the case whether it be on the issue of liability, causation or damages. The most fertile area of defense was typically causation, especially if the plaintiff had prior accidents or pre-existing conditions.

Most of the cases settled before trial at mediation but some cases had to be tried. The great thing about trying civil cases for the defense is that at the end of the day, everyone goes home. Civil cases involved arguments over money and often times it involved swearing contests between expert witnesses such as doctors on whether the plaintiff had sustained or not sustained a permanent injury from an auto accident.

I found defending auto negligence cases very easy after defending criminal cases and saving defendants from the death penalty. The most challenging part of being a corporate claim litigation counsel was staying on top of your case load and meeting numerous reporting deadlines for correspondences with claim representatives and insureds. At the same time you had to manage your pretrial discovery and prepare your cases for trial and mediation.

Pretrial discovery entailed taking depositions or sworn statements from the plaintiffs and other witnesses in the case and responding to other discovery request from the plaintiff's attorney such as interrogatories – (which are questions directed to your client and expert witnesses), request for production of documents, and requests for admissions to certain facts which will avoid the necessity for proof at trial.

The most enjoyable part of being a claim litigation counsel for me was being in trial. Initially, I was given several more challenging cases to try as it seemed the claim office wanted to see how I would perform in trial. It was a "guinea pig" mentality. It was not long before State Farm recognized by trial success with announcement of Jim Pierce Day at the Regional Office in Winter Haven.

While at State Farm, I compiled a trial record of twenty wins, four losses and one hung jury. I won five consecutive cases before I lost my first case. I loved to try cases and would stay up endless hours during the night reviewing evidence and composing closing arguments for the jury. I approached every case as one that I could win.

Chapter Twenty

Rejuvenation

Anointed and Appointed

"For there is no power but of God: the powers
that be are ordained of God." Romans 13:1

On March 12, 1997, I received my first promotion and the salary increase with State Farm. Promotions and salary increases kept coming until I had reached and surpassed my salary level at the Public Defender's office. By the time I reached my ten year anniversary with State Farm, I was earning well beyond six figures. I had proven that I could successfully defend State Farm and its insureds. My career was going very well. One day during the fall of 2006, I received a call from Danell. Whenever Danell called me, I knew she was doing something good for someone or for some cause. "So are you going to put your name in for Judge Grube's seat," she said. "I think you should and you would do a great job."

Dr. Miller's inquiries about my pursuit of the bench and Danell's prodding rejuvenated my interest in becoming a member of the judiciary. I was about to enter the perfect storm. After ten years with State Farm, another nomination opportunity occurred for me when Judge Grube decided to retire. I firmly believe that whatever God has for you, is for you. The Lord has a master plan and often times we may tinker with it and stray off the path but He will get you where he wants you to be.

Once again, it was time to make a choice to take a chance and change my life.

More than ten years had passed since the poison pen letter and I had added 25 civil jury trials and State Farm Corporate Litigation Counsel to my resume. I completed the application and hoped to get an interview with the (JNC). The commission received 47 applications for their consideration and would recommend six names to Governor Bush for his review and appointment. I began the process of having colleagues write and call the Chairperson of the committee and the other members on the 6th Judicial Circuit JNC. I expected to get an interview but what would happen after that was uncertain. After spending hours completing the Application for Pinellas County Court, I forwarded it to the members of the Judicial Nominating Commission.

My interview with the JNC was scheduled on my birthday and this seemed like a sign that something really good was about to happen for me. Like the rest of the candidates, I wanted to make a favorable impression on the JNC. I decided that I would wear a Tuxedo to the interview. This was a risky move as it may not be well received by all of the commissioners. I wanted to distinguish myself from my competitors. It is important to dress for success and I entered the interview with a smile and confidence.

Regardless of what was going to happen, I was happy with State Farm and loved being a trial attorney so this interview was not life or death for me. I felt good about my networking prior to the interview and believed that my work history and success in both criminal and civil practice was as good as the other 47 applicants.

I received abundant support from so many wonderful people in the local community. I was blessed to have the support of Pastor William F. Sherman and the members of Mt. Carmel Baptist Church where I served as a deacon. I also received tremendous support from both civil and criminal defense lawyers and my neighbors. I prayed that I would be selected as one of the six nominees to the Governor if it was God's will.

Fortunately, my previous experiences with the interviewing and networking process for appointment helped me. Convincing a majority of the members on the JNC that you should be among the nominees is an interesting process. I was pleased to know that Attorney Larry Hart, was chairperson of the committee. I knew he would appreciate my trial experience with him being a successful litigator and knowing the importance of having judges with trial experience on the bench.

My interpersonal skills would help me leave a favorable impression on the JNC. As I entered the room, and look around for a familiar face, I saw Larry and Cassandra Jackson. Ms. Jackson, an African American woman, had performed my background check. I had done my research on each of the commissioners as they had done research on each of the applicants. When I left the room, I felt confident that the interview had gone well but remembered my previous disappointments.

I had tickets for the George Clinton concert and was heading to the concert in St. Petersburg when I received the phone call from Cassandra. I had been selected as one of the six nominees for consideration by Florida Governor Jeb Bush. I was overwhelmed with joy!

The political battle for the appointment would now move to the state government level. While I was swollen with joy, my thoughts were now about the other five nominees. Who are they? What can I bring to the table that they don't have and how do I convince Governor Jeb Bush to select me? Long ago, I learned in my political science class under the tutelage of Dr. Jake Miller that politics is all about "who gets what, when, where, and how." I had a renewed energy and confidence that this was my time.

In politics and in the job market, it's not always what you know but most times who you know that makes a difference. When you have the knowledge and know the right people, your chances of getting a job position or political appointment improves greatly. I was fortunate that through my career as an attorney, I had made some great friends and never burned any bridges.

There were several attorneys who played a significant role in my journey to the bench. There were many who wrote letters on my behalf to both the JNC and the Governor's office expressing their confidence in me and belief that I had the judicial temperament necessary to be a good judge. I am grateful to each of them.

There were also those who were able to move and shake the powers that be and influenced the Governor to choose me above my five opponents. Darryl Rouson was one of those movers and shakers. I have always admired Florida State Senator Darryl Rouson's ability as a lawyer and community leader. He is one of the most articulate and dynamic attorneys I have ever met. He was the first African-American attorney to serve as an Assistant State Attorney in the 6th Judicial Circuit.

Rouson is a real life example of how a setback is a setup for a comeback. Rouson was able to overcome various personal and professional adversities along with phenomenal family issues. After returning to St. Petersburg in 1998, we met for lunch and reconnected.

Rouson's activism in the community and his law practice often involved his passions for civil rights and battle against substance abuse. In November 2000, he won an election as president of the St. Petersburg Chapter of the NAACP. By early 2003, the NAACP under Rouson's leadership achieved a number of milestones in meeting its goals.

Pinellas County created a program to help small businesses owned by minorities. The first African American was appointed to the *St. Petersburg Times* board of directors. The Pinellas County Sheriff's Office appointed its first black captain. The school board hired more African-American subcontractors for the construction of Gibbs High School.

In September 2005, Rouson joined the Republican Party and supported Charlie Crist for his successful bid to become governor. It certainly helped my cause to have Rouson pulling on the Governor Bush's coat tail after being nominated for appointment.

On the day following my nomination, I was in the office at 5:30 a.m. blasting e-mails to all my supporters and urging them to write the Governor. I was determined that none of my opponents would out work me in my pursuit for the bench. I called everyone I knew that could exert influence in Tallahassee in support of my appointment. I was fortunate to have the support of former Assistant Public Defender and prominent civil attorney, Jim Stearns. Jim was in the felony division of the Public Defender's Office when I was in the misdemeanor division.

Jim was another "mover and shaker" on the local level. Jim was kind enough to put on a luncheon for me at Al Fresco's in downtown Dunedin and invited the Mayor of Dunedin, Representative Susan Latvala and many other local elected officials to support my pursuit of the bench. Jim humbly served on various boards for numerous organizations and gave back to the community in so many different ways. Jim's success as a prominent attorney with impeccable character, calm temperament, would result in his election to the 6th Judicial Circuit Court with opposition.

I was also very blessed to receive the support of the late Cecil King, a long time Black Republican who knew and was well respected by Governor Bush. Arlington Nunn, my fraternity brother and fellow deacon, was instrumental in helping me gain the support of Mr. King. Arlington and I had completed deacon training school together at Mount Carmel Baptist Church. Arlington was a prominent figure in the Pinellas County School System where he was the Director of Operations before retiring.

I was able to obtain the support of the Mayor of Clearwater, Frank Hibbard, and some of the other mayors in the surrounding municipalities. I was also fortunate to have the support of the attorneys within my firm and our managing attorney, Kevin Korth.

Kevin was also a "mover and shaker" and was able to convince the State Farm powers that existed in Tallahassee to support my nomination to the Governor. Kevin was definitely one of my avid supporters, even though it meant he would be losing me as an attorney within his office. Kevin did everything he could for me and I am grateful for having the opportunity to work under his supervision and learn the practice of insurance defense law.

The other nominees included five other males. Carl Brody was an African American attorney who had worked in the Pinellas County Attorney's office for many years. Carl was also my fraternity brother and had solid support from the St. Petersburg community. Similarly, Carl was also President of the St. Petersburg Chapter of Alpha Phi Alpha Fraternity and I was President of the Clearwater Chapter of Alpha Phi Alpha, Fraternity. We held each other in high regard as fraternity brothers and had often exchanged pleasantries at our fraternity's Annual Scholarship Golf Tournaments fundraisers. Carl's experience was limited to his work in the Pinellas County Attorney's Office and he had not practiced criminal law.

Matt Kidder was a prominent criminal defense attorney and former state attorney. Matt and I were also friends and had mutual respect for each other. Matt would make a great judge and he has been nominated on numerous of occasions.

Glenn Martin was an Assistant State Attorney and former police officer. Glenn had a remarkable and successful career in the State Attorney's Office trying murder cases, white collar crimes and other felony cases. Glenn had not practiced civil law.

Jack Day was a prominent civil attorney and a good friend of Danell. I had not met Jack and did not know what his qualifications were. Jack was a Board Certified Civil Attorney. I was a Board Certified Criminal Trial Attorney. Board Certification was recognition that the attorney has met certain standards, passed a written examination, and is a specialist in a particular area of practice. Jack did not have any criminal trial practice experience.

Thomas Minkoff was a civil attorney and represented the Pinellas Republican Party. Of all the candidates, he was the most formidable. Tom was an active member of the Republican Party and had connections to the Governor's Office and local politicians. When I met Thomas Minkoff, he had a glow of confidence about him that immediately made me feel that I had no chance of keeping him from receiving the nomination.

Tom had the political connections and contributed to campaigns and I had not. I had 22 years of trial experience as a criminal defense attorney and insurance defense litigator. My record spoke for itself but I faced an opponent who was politically connected. What now?

I prayed that God would help me to reach the bench. I needed divine intervention and it arrived when an article in the St. Petersburg reported that Tom had made a contribution to the campaign fund of a JNC member. This revelation raised concerns of bias and improper influence between a JNC member and potential nominee. All of sudden Tom's glow of confidence became a glimmer of hope for me. Would Governor Bush appoint me or would he disregard the potential conflict of interest?

In order to get the nomination, I had to do some serious political networking. My first and most important connection was to meet with the Chair-person of the Pinellas County Republican Party, Paul Bedinghaus. My meeting with Paul was monumental and I am greatly indebted to him for pointing me in the right direction. I told Paul about my experience meeting Governor Bush in 1994 when he visited the Public Defender's office during his first unsuccessful bid to become Florida's Governor. I mentioned that I had attended a campaign activity for Governor Bush in Tallahassee with other supporters from the Public Defender's Office. My time with Paul was well spent and provided invaluable insight for the upcoming interview with the Governor's office.

Before I knew it, several months had passed from the night I received word on my nomination. On February 17, 2006, President George W. Bush was in Tampa delivering remarks on the Global War on Terror to citizens of the Tampa, Florida area inside the Port of Tampa cruise ship terminal and participating in a briefing by CENTCOM AND SOCOM Commanders at MacDill Air Force Base. He had been joined by Governor Bush.

I was suffering from the flu and had taken a sick day to recover when I received a phone call from the Governor' s office General

Counsel's Office. I was told that the Governor was considering me for an appointment but needed some clarification about a child abuse allegation. An anonymous allegation had been made more than 15 years ago about our children being neglected. Fortunately for me this allegation was investigated by Department of Health and Human Services and was determined to be unfounded. Basically, the allegation was that our kids were outside riding their bikes without supervision. We lived on a cul de sac and it was not unusual for our kids to be outside riding their bikes while we were inside the house. Fortunately, I had kept the written findings regarding this allegation as part of my records. I never imagined I would need this documentation for any reason but I had retained it in my records. I faxed the information to the general counsel's office and was back home eating a tuna sandwich when the phone rang. The voice on the line asked, "Is this Mr. James Pierce?"

I responded, "Yes sir, speaking."

The reply was, "Please stay on the line, Governor Bush would like to speak to you."

My heart beat seemed to stop, and then I heard the voice of the Governor.

"I hear you want to be a judge?"

"Yes sir," I responded.

Then the Governor said, "From this day forward you are a Judge and remember what you said in your application."

I was in shock and for a moment could not remember what I had said in my application but simply responded, "Thank you sir and I will do my best to make you proud of my appointment." Hallelujah and praise God were the first words out of my mouth. My journey from the field to the court had been accomplished and I was anxious to share the good news with everyone who had made my dream come true. The journey from the field to the court was over except for the shouting and celebrating which would come in due time. I remembered the words in my application:

Despite the fact that I was raised in a low income, single parent home, I have always strived to be the best person that I can be. At age ten, I performed farm labor to pay for my necessities and continued that same work ethic through college and law school. I have excelled in all facets of my professional career. Like most folk, I have experienced highs and lows in the journey we call life but I continue to strive to live it to its fullest. If selected as a Pinellas County Judge, I will work diligently to perform the duties required of the office and strive to create an environment where justice rolls down like a mighty river. I will insure that attorneys, parties, witnesses, jurors, and court personnel are treated respectfully and fairly on their day in court.

The Honorable James V. Pierce – Sixth Judicial Circuit Court

Made in the USA
Columbia, SC
16 July 2019